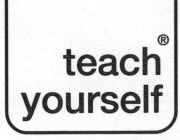

teach yourself ®

successful selling

D0869230

successful selling

roger brooksbank

Launched in 1938, the **teach yourself** series grew rapidly in response to the world's wartime needs. Loved and trusted by over 50 million readers, the series has continued to respond to society's changing interests and passions and now, 70 years on, includes over 500 titles, from Arabic and Beekeeping to Yoga and Zulu. What would you like to learn?

be where you want to be with **teach yourself**

For UK order enquiries: please contact Bookpoint Ltd, 130 Milton Park, Abingdon, Oxon OX14 4SB. Telephone: +44 (0) 1235 827720. Fax: +44 (0) 1235 400454. Lines are open 09.00–17.00, Monday to Saturday, with a 24-hour message answering service. Details about our titles and how to order are available at www.teachyourself.co.uk

For USA order enquiries: please contact McGraw-Hill Customer Services, PO Box 545, Blacklick, OH 43004-0545, USA. Telephone: 1-800-722-4726. Fax: 1-614-755-5645.

For Canada order enquiries: please contact McGraw-Hill Ryerson Ltd, 300 Water St, Whitby, Ontario L1N 9B6, Canada. Telephone: 905 430 5000. Fax: 905 430 5020.

Long renowned as the authoritative source for self-guided learning – with more than 50 million copies sold worldwide – the **teach yourself** series includes over 500 titles in the fields of languages, crafts, hobbies, business, computing and education.

British Library Cataloguing in Publication Data: a catalogue record for this title is available from the British Library.

Library of Congress Catalog Card Number: on file.

First published in UK 2009 by Hodder Education, part of Hachette UK, 338 Euston Road, London, NW1 3BH.

First published in US 2009 by The McGraw-Hill Companies, Inc.

This edition published 2009.

The **teach yourself** name is a registered trade mark of Hodder Headline.

Copyright © 2009 Roger Brooksbank

Typeset by Transet Limited, Coventry, England.
Printed in Great Britain for Hodder Education, an Hachette UK Company, 338 Euston Road, London NW1 3BH, by CPI Cox & Wyman, Reading, Berkshire RG1 8EX.

The publisher has used its best endeavours to ensure that the URLs for external websites referred to in this book are correct and active at the time of going to press. However, the publisher and the author have no responsibility for the websites and can make no guarantee that a site will remain live or that the content will remain relevant, decent or appropriate.

Hachette UK's policy is to use papers that are natural, renewable and recyclable products and made from wood grown in sustainable forests. The logging and manufacturing processes are expected to conform to the environmental regulations of the country of origin.

Impression number   10 9 8 7 6 5 4 3 2 1
Year   2013 2012 2011 2010 2009

contents

preface

In a challenging business environment, what do you think is the X factor that differentiates that small group of top-performing salespeople in your industry? Do they work harder than you? Probably not. Are they more self-motivated and self-disciplined than you? Hardly likely. Could it be that they're more knowledgeable about the features and benefits of their products and services? I seriously doubt it. OK, they must be more experienced then – is that it? Not necessarily.

Would you agree with me that while all these factors are important prerequisites for sales success, none of them gets even close to explaining the true difference between an ordinary salesperson and a top performer?

Let's make no mistake about it. The X factor is a five-letter word: skill. It's a little word that makes a big difference; all the difference, in fact, to a salesperson's performance.

There's no getting away from it. The best way to increase your sales performance is to focus on improving your selling skills, and this book will help you do just that. It provides a concise description of 52 specific selling skills that are essential for any salesperson who sells face-to-face. Best of all, each skill comes with a 'call-to-action' in the form of a *skill acquisition exercise*. These exercises provide a starting point for taking the skills off the pages of this book and translating them into your day-to-day selling.

You'll find this book quick and easy to read. What's more, it's a book that you can refer to again and again as a source of new ideas and inspiration. So, study it, use it, apply it … and watch yourself begin to close more sales!

Roger Brooksbank

acknowledgements

My sincere thanks go to all of the following for making a contribution in one way or another towards the writing of this book: John Clarke, Jeremy Edwards, Brian Marshall, Steve Kane, Nathalie Giraud, Laurent Besnard-Chantecler, Mike Bottomley, Paul McLaughlin, Fiona McLaughlin, Peter Jones, David Kirby, James McIntosh, Michelle Pinkerton, Michelle Smith, Ning Zhang, Andrew Morgan, Richard Morgan, Zahed Subhan, David Taylor, Alastair Marshall, Sophie Cotter, Mark Lytham, Sally Board, Ed Board, Margaret Brooksbank, Kathryn Borg, Ron Garland, Scott Koslow, Trisha Koslow, Lorraine Friend, Marilynne Burton, Quentin Somerville, Neil Lynn, Michele Lynn, Mary FitzPatrick, Merryn Dunsmuir, Renee Railton, Deborah Callahan, Janine Evans and Nikki Leonard.

I would also like to thank my favourite 'selling gurus' – Tom Hopkins, Brian Tracey, Linda Richardson, Robin Fielder, John Fenton and Richard Denny – none of whom I know personally but whose books have sharpened my understanding of professional selling.

Last but not least, special thanks also go to the thousands of salespeople who have attended my sales seminars, training workshops and coaching programmes over the years. It is their positive feedback that inspired me to publish this book.

about the author

Roger Brooksbank has a PhD in strategic marketing, and is an internationally-known author, trainer and speaker in the areas of marketing planning, business promotion, entrepreneurship and professional selling.

Roger has previous experience as a salesperson, sales manager, marketing director and business owner in the UK, and he has also worked extensively in Europe and Australasia as an independent marketing consultant.

Roger is currently an associate professor of marketing with the prestigious University of Waikato Management School in Hamilton, New Zealand.

For further information, please visit **www.rogerbrooksbank.com** or to contact Roger directly, email **roger@rogerbrooksbank.com**

introduction

Is this book for you?

If you are a professional salesperson selling your company's products and services face-to-face with customers, or if you are responsible for training a regional or national sales force, then yes, this book is for you.

Five main skill areas – OIMCO™

On the basis of my extensive involvement in sales training over the past 25 years, I have found that the process of face-to-face selling can be usefully broken down into five sequential phases, or 'skill areas', otherwise known as the O I M C O ™ model:

- Opening
- Interviewing
- Matching
- Closing
- Objection-handling.

Most importantly, I have observed that whenever a salesperson focuses their efforts on improving their skills in these areas, success inevitably follows. So, let's take a closer look at each of these five areas:

The opening phase

This begins the moment a salesperson comes face-to-face with a customer. During this phase a salesperson needs the skills to create a favourable first impression and to set the scene for a businesslike and mutually beneficial conversation to take place.

The interviewing phase

A salesperson cannot prescribe a solution for their customer until they have thoroughly diagnosed their buying situation. So, during this phase of the selling process, a salesperson needs to employ a variety of interviewing skills in order to find out all about their customer's specific needs and wants, and to uncover the key benefits that they are really looking for.

The matching phase

Once a customer's specific requirements have been established, a salesperson needs the skills to match, as closely as possible, that customer's needs and wants to the benefits of their product or service.

The closing phase

Closing is about helping the customer to make up their mind. During this phase of the process a salesperson needs to be able to draw on a wide range of skills for getting the customer's agreement to go ahead with making their purchase, and for ensuring that they are left feeling positive about their decision.

The objection-handling phase

This phase is triggered whenever the customer responds negatively in some way to a salesperson's offer. This occurs when there's an area of 'perceived mismatch' in the customer's mind – a mismatch between what he or she wants and their understanding of what is on offer. So, during this phase of the sale, a salesperson needs the skills to be able to handle the customer's objection to their complete satisfaction and, whenever possible, turn it around into a closing opportunity.

As you can see, in order to progress successfully through each of the five phases of the O I M C O ™ model, a salesperson must be able to call upon an array of selling skills at each phase. The purpose of this book is to help you to acquire these skills.

I've divided the book into five chapters, with each chapter corresponding to one of the five phases of the O I M C O ™ model, as shown in the diagram opposite. In each chapter I'll take you through a number of specific selling skills that are essential to becoming an expert 'opener', 'interviewer', 'matcher', 'closer' and 'objection-handler'. In total the book covers 52 skills, numbered 1 through to 52 for ease of reference. Each skill is written in a straightforward fashion and clearly spells out the how-to-do-its, concluding with a call to action in the form of a *skill acquisition exercise*. These exercises are important because they provide a starting point for taking the skills off the pages of this book and putting them into practice in your day-to-day selling.

The OIMCO™ model of face-to-face selling

Opening phase

Set the scene for a businesslike and mutually beneficial conversation to take place between you and the customer.

↓

Interviewing phase

Find out all about the customer's specific needs and wants, and uncover the key benefits that they are really looking for.

↓

Matching phase

Match the customer's needs and wants as closely as possible to the benefits of your product or service offer.

↓

Closing phase

Get the customer's agreement to go ahead, and leave them feeling positive about their purchase decision.

↓

Objection-handling phase

Handle the customer's objection to their complete satisfaction and, if possible, turn it around into a closing opportunity.

At this point you're probably wondering: 'By how much will this book enable me to improve?' Well, of course I can't give you a straight answer to that question because it all depends on your current level of knowledge and expertise. Certainly, not all the 52 skills will necessarily be of equal value or even new to you. However, I can promise you one thing: my book will surprise you if you let it. Providing you read it with an open mind, with a willingness to learn and, above all, with a willingness to try out new ideas and to change your selling habits, you will become a better salesperson and you will close more sales. I've worked with salespeople from some of the world's leading organizations and I've seen it happen. If it works for them, it can work for you too.

Getting the most from this book

It isn't just a convenient coincidence that I've included the same number of selling skills in this book as there are weeks in a year. It's designed to be read S-L-O-W-L-Y – with the intention of acquiring one skill per week for a year. That's all. Except that's not all. Let me explain …

Don't just read it, do something!

This book isn't just for reading – it's for acting upon! In fact, the words on its pages amount to only a tiny fraction of the book's true value. It's what you *do* as a result of reading it that counts. So this is my suggested weekly game plan:

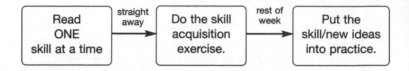

Focus your attention solely on reading through one skill at a time; this will take just a few minutes. Then do the *skill acquisition exercise* right away, while it's still fresh in your mind. Doing this exercise is important because it forces you to think about what you could do differently that might help you to sell better. Then for the rest of your working week, take the opportunity to try putting your new ideas into practice during real selling situations, using a process of trial and error to see what works best.

Work systematically through all 52 skills

Regardless of your current level of knowledge and expertise, for optimal results I strongly recommend that you work systematically through all 52 skills in this book. Start with Skill 1 and just keep on going until you've finished Skill 52. Even though you might already be a seasoned professional, and highly proficient in many of the more 'basic' selling skills, please don't be tempted to skip any of them. Just as the world's top musicians, golfers or dancers never stop working on honing their basic skills, neither do the world's top salespeople and therefore neither should you. By all means spend less time working on some selling skills than on others as appropriate, but please don't short-change yourself. Go through the whole book.

Get yourself a study buddy

A 'study buddy' is another salesperson with whom you join forces as a learning partner. If you can work through this book together, you'll learn a lot more and you'll have more fun doing it. Two heads are better than one, so work closely together comparing notes, providing mutual support and encouragement, and exchanging ideas, knowledge and experience. The ideal study buddy is another member of your sales team who sells the same products and services as you do. However, if this isn't possible, a good choice is any salesperson you know who sells non-competing products or services and who, just like you, wants to keep on improving.

About the audio programme

An audio programme accompanies this book. The audio programme is structured in accordance with the O I M C O ™ model and contains 22 top tips for successful face-to-face selling. Presented in a lively, fast-moving and entertaining format, it's ideal for listening to in the car between sales calls. In this context it will provide plenty of food for thought when reflecting back on how well you performed during your last sales call. It will also be a timely source of inspiration and ideas in preparation for the next one you're about to make. Used in this way, you'll find it's a great catalyst for self-improvement, either as a stand-alone resource or as the perfect companion to this book.

01
opening-phase selling skills

In this chapter you will learn:
- how to set the scene for a businesslike and mutually beneficial conversation to take place between you and the customer.

Opening phase
Set the scene for a businesslike and mutually beneficial conversation to take place between you and the customer.

↓

Interviewing phase
Find out all about the customer's specific needs and wants, and uncover the key benefits that they are really looking for.

↓

Matching phase
Match the customer's needs and wants as closely as possible to the benefits of your product or service offer.

↓

Closing phase
Get the customer's agreement to go ahead, and leave them feeling positive about their purchase decision.

↓

Objection-handling phase
Handle the customer's objection to their complete satisfaction and, if possible, turn it around into a closing opportunity.

1 Go through a set-up routine

Picture this. You're fully prepared for an appointment with a prospective customer. You've arrived at their offices with five minutes to spare, parked your car and walked into their reception area. The receptionist tells you that they will be with you shortly and invites you to take a seat. Then it happens. Your mind slips out of the present. Perhaps there is a lot happening in your life and there are other things on your mind. Maybe your head is swimming with nervous anticipation or self-doubt. Whatever the reason, the result is that when the time comes to greet the customer your mind is elsewhere and not focused on the task at hand. Sound familiar?

If you've ever watched an Olympic gymnast or a professional golfer in action you'll know exactly what I mean by a 'set-up routine' (or a 'habitual ritual' as it's sometimes called). Immediately before the gymnast performs a discipline or the golfer hits a shot he or she performs a little ritual that helps to focus the mind and put them in 'the zone' – a place of total concentration and mindfulness in relation to what they are about to do. Of course the routine itself will be different for a salesperson but the principle is the same. Going through a set-up routine in the few moments before meeting a prospective customer is a habit you can acquire to ensure that you're completely focused on performing to the best of your ability every time.

Here are some examples of the set-up routines often used by top salespeople:

- Read through any notes you have made relating to the customer you're about to see.
- Access the 'little voice' that's inside your head and use positive self-talk to remind yourself of the value of your offer to the customer.
- Rehearse the exact words you're going to use when greeting the customer by quietly repeating them several times to yourself.
- Do some slow deep-breathing exercises to centre yourself in the moment and become perfectly calm and collected.

Whenever you have a particularly important sale coming up, I'd recommend a set-up routine called 'mental movie-making'. It works like this: by drawing on the databanks of your memory you already have the ability to make a 'mental movie' of any one of thousands of past experiences, and in such detail that you can quite literally 're-live' that experience inside your head – right? Well, imagine that instead of making a mental movie of the past, you make one of the future – a movie relating to the next sales presentation that you're about to make. That's when mental movie-making can really work for you. By projecting an up-coming sales scenario onto the screen of your mind and making a movie of it, you can 'live out' the experience just as you want it to happen, thereby effectively conditioning yourself for a successful outcome.

Here's how to do it. First, visualize yourself, in detail, successfully 'acting out' your part as the consummate professional salesperson. Second, add the 'sound track', so that inside your head you can hear every single piece of the dialogue between you and your customer, just the way you want it to unfold. Third, add the emotion, so that you can really feel the sense of elation and success you're going to experience as you visualize the sale moving along towards the customer happily deciding to buy. Fourth, now that you have the finished version of your mental movie (complete with moving pictures, soundtrack and emotion), it's important that you 'imprint' it by playing it over and over in your mind prior to going into your next sale. The more you can 'live out' a successful selling experience just as you want it to happen, the more likely it is that it will become your reality.

In developing your set-up routine, do understand that what works for someone else will not necessarily work for you. Everyone must develop their own uniquely personal routine. Use a process of trial and error to find one that just 'feels right' and works for you. While a set-up routine is no substitute for proper preparation and pre-call planning, in those few crucial moments before meeting a customer it's a great way to de-clutter your mind, eliminate negative thinking, banish last-minute nerves and effectively 'program' yourself for a successful outcome.

Skill acquisition exercise

Develop a set-up routine that will put you in 'the zone' before every sales presentation. Test it, fine-tune it, ritualize it, and turn it into a success habit.

2 Project your professionalism

First impressions are formed in an instant. Yet their effects can last for a lifetime. Even as you walk towards a new customer, long before you are close enough to shake their hand or engage in conversation, you will have announced your credentials as a professional salesperson simply by the way you look. Just as a book is judged by its cover, in those first few seconds a customer will judge you on the basis of three visual cues:

- the clothes you wear
- your body language
- your aura.

Let's take a closer look at each of these three interrelated aspects of the image you are projecting to your customers:

The clothes you wear

The very first thing a customer will notice about you is how you are dressed. In deciding what to wear, the key question to ask yourself is: 'How would my customers expect a top professional salesperson in my industry to be dressed?' – and then dress accordingly. Within these parameters, however, there are a number of general guidelines to bear in mind:

- It's better to dress up than down.
- Avoid excessively brightly coloured clothes because they can be too distracting. You want a customer to be focused on your face and on what you're saying, rather than on your clothes! In particular, avoid wearing bright red because in a face-to-face selling situation it has all the wrong connotations – it spells 'stop' and is too aggressive.
- Pay close attention to the standard of your personal grooming.
- Pay equally close attention to your choice of accessories such as the type and style of briefcase, handbag or hold-all you choose to carry. It's important that accessories complement your overall look.
- If in doubt about any aspect of your appearance, look to your seniors as role models.

Your body language

The way you move, including your gestures, postures and facial expressions is the next thing your customer will notice. Most experts agree that the non-verbal signals a person communicates through their body language are at least as important as the messages they convey verbally. So, as a salesperson meeting up with a customer for the first time, you should aim to convey openness, enthusiasm and co-operation. This can be achieved by ensuring that your jacket is unbuttoned, that you are smiling frequently, maintaining an upright upper body posture and making plenty of direct eye contact. Above all, as you walk towards a customer, put a spring in your step!

Your aura

Your aura can be defined as the invisible 'energy' or 'vibes' that surround your body and radiate outwards from it. Make no mistake about it: despite being invisible to the naked eye, upon meeting you for the first time the vast majority of customers will very quickly sense your aura as being either self-centred or customer-centred. Far from being something that just 'is', as many salespeople seem to believe, the aura you project is almost entirely within your control because it springs directly from the attitude that you bring to your job. Fundamentally, a self-centred attitude is epitomized by the stereotypical fast-talking, manipulative salesperson with pound signs in their eyes and shark's jaws for teeth – the kind of salesperson whose only real goal is to satisfy their own needs and wants by making a sale at any cost. In sharp contrast, a customer-centred attitude is the very essence of the modern professional salesperson whose primary goals are to satisfy their customers' needs and wants, and to gain repeat business and referrals through building mutually beneficial long-term relationships. The choice is all yours.

Skill acquisition exercise

On the screen of your mind, create a detailed picture of what a typical customer in your industry would expect a top professional salesperson to look like in terms of their standard of dress, body language and aura. Now stand in front of a full-length mirror and compare this mental image with what you see reflected in the mirror. Ask yourself: in what ways could I improve?

3 Do the handshake one-two-three-four

In a business setting where a handshake is the usual form of greeting between a buyer and seller, doing the 'handshake one-two-three-four' is an excellent habit to acquire. It means you will always be making the most of the opportunity a handshake presents for creating a favourable first impression and building some initial rapport with your customers. So, when shaking hands, there are four things to remember:

One-two-three-four

Look the customer directly in the eye; not just in the general direction of their eyes, but right into the pupils of their eyes. When you do this it usually only takes one or two split seconds before both you and your new customer experience a brief 'twinkle' response in the pupils of each other's eyes. According to human behaviour experts, at this instant a powerful human bonding process takes place that can have a profound effect on the way people instinctively relate to one another.

One-two-three-four

Make sure you offer a handshake with a straight, firm grip that's neither too firm nor too limp. This will convey an unspoken message to your new customer that you respect him or her as your equal. Above all, avoid the classic 'I want to dominate you' handshake – shaking too vigorously, applying a vice-like grip, or tilting and rolling your hand so that it's over the top of your customer's hand. Incidentally, if your customer shakes your hand this way, a good method of 'neutralizing' it is to briefly clasp their forearm with your other hand. This double-handed response is usually just enough to let them know that you perceive yourself as their equal, not their subordinate.

One-two-three-four

Play the name game. During the act of shaking hands, take the opportunity for personalizing your relationship by asking if you can call your customer by their first name. The best way to do this is to first give your customer permission to call you by your first name before asking for theirs. For example, you might say:

Hi, I'm Roger Brooksbank. Please call me Roger ... and may I call you John?

One-two-three-four

Once you have the customer's permission to use their first name, you can conclude the handshake by thanking him or her for taking the time to see you:

It's good to meet you, John, and thanks for taking the time to see me today.

Successfully executing the handshake one-two-three-four provides you with the necessary springboard to launch into conducting the rest of your conversation in a businesslike yet friendly manner. This is important because when all is said and done, people don't do business with a department, a company or an organization. People do business with people.

Skill acquisition exercise

Practise the handshake one-two-three-four routine with a colleague or friend until it becomes a natural part of your communication style whenever you meet a customer for the first time.

---

4 Introduce your company as a 'perfect partner'

Before finding out exactly what you have to offer, most new customers are going to need a little reassurance that your company is the 'right' kind of company to be dealing with. Think of it as being a bit like dating. In exactly the way a young single person is looking for a perfect life-partner, so too a customer is seeking a perfect business partner; for instance, one that has an established track record, is financially secure, or is of a certain size, reputation and standing. That's why during the opening phase of the sale it's wise to say a few words to introduce your company. Simply highlight those aspects of dealing with your company that you feel will be of greatest appeal to your new customer. In other words, treat it as an opportunity to build some rapport between you. Most importantly, keep your company introduction brief and well rehearsed so that it trips easily off the tongue. Above all, when telling the customer about your company, make sure you sound enthusiastic! For example, if you were selling to a local, family-owned business, you might say something like this:

We're a family-owned business with a reputation for taking great pride in what we do, and we've been based in Weatherfield for over 10 years now … very much like your own company, Michael.

Bear in mind that from a customer's point of view your company is not the sum total of the business partnership under consideration. As your company's salesperson, you yourself also come as part and parcel of the package on offer! So, after introducing your company it usually pays to say a few extra words of self-introduction. This should not be too elaborate. Just a couple of well-chosen sentences that will serve to further influence their initial perception of your company and its people as being the 'right' kind of business partner. For example, you might simply say something like this:

… and as for myself, I'm in my fourth year with the company. Currently I have over 90 satisfied customers in the Weatherfield region with whom I work very closely on a regular basis.

In giving a customer a little background information about yourself, always stick to the facts and resist the temptation to be even remotely boastful about your achievements. In exactly the same way as when introducing your company, your aim is simply to highlight what it is about yourself that is likely to be of greatest appeal to your new customer.

Skill acquisition exercise

Write down the exact wording of (a) the best way to introduce your company to a new customer and (b) the best way to give a new customer a little more information about yourself. Rehearse these statements until you can say them naturally and confidently.

---

5 Build STAR-quality rapport

The term 'rapport' refers to a feeling of personal warmth between you and your customer. If you can build some degree of rapport early on in your sales presentation, then it makes it easy to develop even more as the conversation unfolds. This is important because ultimately, customers only want to do business with someone who they think is an 'OK' person and with whom they feel comfortable. Using the word STAR as an acronym, you can become an effective rapport-builder simply by going through the following four-step rapport-building routine with every new customer you meet:

S = Smile at your customer

A smile, as they say, really is the shortest distance between two people! A relaxed and smiling face lightens the atmosphere and makes you much more friendly and approachable. However, make sure that in putting a smile on your face you do so with sincerity. A smile that comes from the heart will signal to your new customer that you have a genuine interest in him or her as a person.

T = Tell your customer something about yourself

The sooner you let your new customer know a little about who you are on a personal level – something about your background, such as where you were born, where you went to school, or where you live – the sooner they will be able to relate to you as a human being and not 'just another' salesperson. Also, they will be more likely to feel some measure of obligation to tell you a little about themselves in return.

A = Ask your customer something about themselves

Enquire about some aspect of your customer's life: their place of birth, family members, favourite holiday destination, interests and pastimes and so on. However, make sure you do so with as much genuine interest as you can muster. A sure-fire way to kill the sale before you even start is to appear to be just going through the motions of making some small talk without really caring about what your customer is saying.

R = Relate to your customer

The real key to being able to build great rapport is to find something, anything at all, that you have in common with your new customer. It might be that you share mutual friends or contacts, mutual sporting interests or a mutual love of the arts. It doesn't really matter what it is just as long as it's something that builds a bridge of understanding that you are indeed similar people in some way.

Although extreme care should be taken not to spend too much time giving your customers the STAR treatment, don't underestimate the effectiveness of this simple little rapport-building routine. The trick is to weave it into your initial conversation with each customer and in such a way that it comes across as a natural part of your communication style.

Skill acquisition exercise

Paying close attention to your use of appropriate body language (gestures, posture, facial expressions etc.) and to your use of an appropriate tone of voice, role-play the STAR rapport-building formula with a colleague or friend.

---

6 Qualify your customer

Have you ever gone through your entire sales presentation only to find out that the person you've been talking to is not the true decision-maker? When this happens, not only is it extremely frustrating but it also means you've wasted a lot of time and risked compromising your professional credibility.

Well, if it's any consolation, I'd wager there are few salespeople who haven't learned the hard way that no matter how well you pre-qualify your prospect as a bona fide customer before setting up an appointment, you should always go through the process of qualifying him or her again when you get there. The fact is, in business-to-business selling there are usually a number of questions well worth asking once you've met up with your customer face-to-face. Here are some example questions to get you thinking:

Once we've concluded our discussions today …

… providing everything is to your complete satisfaction, can you tell me if you're the person who is able to make the final decision?

… what is your role exactly?

… would anyone else be involved?

… what is their role?

... would it be helpful if we included them in our meeting today?

... how does your company's decision-making process work?

... what would be your next step?

The crucial question, and normally the first question you must ask, relates to whether or not the person in front of you has decision-making authority. If the answer is unequivocally in the affirmative, then you probably won't need to ask many more qualifying questions. If, on the other hand, you receive a guarded or negative response, then you'll have to find out more by asking some or even all of the above questions.

Some salespeople worry that by asking such questions they risk offending their customer by implying that he or she might not have sufficient seniority to make a purchase decision. Others doubt the wisdom of asking these questions at all for fear of providing their customer with a ready-made 'escape route' before the meeting even gets started. However, unless you know for sure that the person you've gone to see has sole decision-making authority, the reality is that you can't afford *not* to ask them. By all means, be as tactful as you can with regard to the manner in which you ask your questions, but don't leave these issues hanging in the air because they're not going to go away. You know it and your customer knows it. Indeed, most customers will respect you for tackling these issues up front. Better still, it's precisely because you ask them that they'll be more likely to perceive you as the kind of salesperson who has the experience, industry knowledge and confidence they're looking for. It's what a customer expects of a professional salesperson.

Skill acquisition exercise

Prepare a list of questions that you would feel comfortable in using to qualify your customers when you meet them face-to-face. Practise how you're going to ask these questions in a customer-friendly and non-judgemental manner.

7 Take control of your selling space

Providing you visit your customers at their place of business, at some point within the first few minutes of the opening phase of the sale it is always necessary to make an assessment of the space the customer has set aside for your meeting. Is it going to be conducive to carrying out your presentation and is there anything you should do to improve it?

In carrying out your assessment there are all sorts of environmental factors to look out for, all of which could seriously compromise your chances of delivering a great sales presentation. For example, is there going to be sufficient privacy for your customer? Does it look as though there is going to be a lot of background activity or noise that will be distracting for your customer? Will there be enough desk or table-top space available? Is the seating arranged to your liking? Will it be too warm or too cold to be comfortable, and will there be sufficient ventilation and lighting?

If, having scanned your selling space, you decide it is not as good as it could be, then you should move quickly to do something about it before proceeding with your sales presentation. This is not a time to be faint-hearted! Simply go right ahead and suggest to the customer how you think the conditions for your meeting could be improved, perhaps by rearranging some furniture, opening a window, turning on the lights or whatever. If necessary you could even suggest moving to an adjacent office or ask if there is another room available that would be more suitable. For example, you might say:

> *Since we're going to be exchanging a lot of commercially sensitive information, is there another office we could use that would give us some privacy?*

As long as you put it in such a way that you are obviously showing care and consideration for your customer and acting as much in their best interests as your own, they will usually be only too happy to let you take control of your selling space in this way. In fact, most customers will appreciate your candour and it will probably have the effect of enhancing their perception of your professionalism.

Sometimes your customers will be well versed in the art of 'persuasive buying'. This is something of a double-edged sword. On the one hand it means the space set aside for your meeting will undoubtedly be functional and adequate for your purposes – they will have made sure of that. On the other hand, it also means they will have 'stage-managed' it to their advantage. Commonly referred to as the use of 'territory power', I'm talking about a customer's deliberate use of the familiar surroundings of their office to undermine a salesperson's aspiration levels and to play on any insecurities they might be feeling about their prices being 'too high'. Here's a typical scenario:

Example

As you walk into the customer's office he or she stands up to greet you from behind a huge, expensive-looking desk before sitting back down on a plush swivel chair. In the meantime, you are invited to be seated on the only other chair in the room across the desk. It's a small chair that's less than comfortable, and puts you on a lower level than your customer. Then, as the conversation begins, you notice that he or she is silhouetted against a large window, which makes it very difficult to see the detail of their facial expressions. What's more, you can't help but notice that their desk is littered with your competitors' brochures and price lists ...

Clearly, this sort of situation is designed to intimidate and the customer has purposely left you with very little scope, if any, for influencing your selling environment. So it's important to be able to recognize the use of territory power for what it is and not to let it faze you. It's a buying tactic that only works if you let it, which is why the best way to counter it is to ignore it. While under such circumstances you might not be able to take control of your selling space, you can, at least, control your reaction to it.

Skill acquisition exercise

Imagine the ideal setting in which you would like to be able to conduct all your sales presentations and develop a mental checklist of your 'must have' requirements. Decide how you intend to communicate this to your customers whenever it becomes necessary.

---

8 Use an appropriate attention-grabber

Would you like to double your sales in the next twelve months?

Have you ever heard of an attention-grabber? Yes, you're right. I just used one! Admittedly it was not a very original one perhaps, but nonetheless it was an attention-grabber.

Just about every model of selling states that before you can sell anything to anybody you must first get their undivided attention. So an 'attention-grabber' is a device for doing just that. It's something you ask, tell, show, give or, better still, involve the customer in doing, which captures their attention, arouses their curiosity and makes them want to learn more about what you have to offer. Here's an example:

Example

Tom sells refrigerated display cabinets to small convenience stores. He walks into a store and introduces himself to the owner, then takes a 1 m^2 piece of folded-up fluorescent yellow paper out of his inside pocket and proceeds to unfold it, fold by fold, in front of the store owner. Then he puts it down on the floor by the counter and gets the owner to stand on it, before asking a question that goes something like this:

Tell me, how would you like that spare piece of floor space you're standing on to earn you an extra £3500 next year?

So let's take a closer look at the main types of attention-grabber that are typically used by top salespeople. As you can see, your choice of an appropriate attention-grabber is limited only by your imagination:

- a benefit-loaded question

  How would you like to cut your telephone bill by up to 45 per cent next month?

- a striking factual statement

  Did you know that, according to the latest government statistics ...

- a reference to someone they know

  Fred Smith from the XYZ Company suggested I should see you because ...

- a reference to a news item

  Congratulations! I see from this month's trade magazine that your company has just won a big export order ...

- an unexpected gift

  On behalf of the ABC Corporation please accept this small gift ... it's yours to keep with our compliments ...

- an unusual photograph or exhibit of some kind

  Take a look at this ...

- a dramatic mini-demonstration

  Here ... drop this piece of our super-strength shatterproof glass and watch it bounce ...

In choosing to use an attention-grabber, always remember that it must be both *appropriate* to the nature of your product or service and *credible* to your target customers. For example, if you sell merchant banking services to company directors in the boardroom then it would hardly be appropriate to use an attention-grabber that was too 'flashy' or too rich in entertainment value. Another important consideration is that you must plan ahead. Just as with any other selling tool, the success with which you deploy an attention-grabber will always be dependent on a flawless execution – and that can only be achieved by meticulous planning, preparation and rehearsal.

Skill acquisition exercise

Devise an appropriate attention-grabber that you could use at a certain point during the opening phase of your sales presentation. Practise carrying it out.

---

9 Set an agenda

You have just met your prospective customer. You've introduced yourself and made a good first impression. Next, you've been through the ritual of chatting a little and have taken the opportunity of building some rapport. So now what? Well, now is the time to take control of the conversation by providing the customer with a 'road-map' of how you intend to proceed. In other words, you should suggest an outline agenda for the meeting and get the customer's agreement to it so that you can get started in a businesslike way. There's no need for anything too elaborate. Simply say you'd like to cover this, then that, and so on, in order to make the best use of your time together. For example, you could say something like this:

> *Susan, I want to make sure that we make the very best use of the time we've set aside for our meeting today. So I'd like to start off by asking you a few questions to find out all about you and your requirements. Then providing I think we can help, I'd like to explore with you exactly how we could go about doing that ... does that sound OK to you?*

If you sell a highly customized and/or a particularly complex product or service, it might be preferable to provide your customer with a preprepared written agenda that itemizes all the key topics for discussion. At the appropriate time you simply hand it to your customer while saying something like this:

> *Since we have a lot of items to discuss today, I've taken the liberty of preparing a brief outline agenda ... please Susan ... take a moment to read through it and let me know if you think it looks OK ...*

Setting an agenda for your meeting with a customer has a number of advantages. Not only does it come across as being highly professional but it also provides you with an element of control throughout the rest of the meeting so that whenever necessary you are able to refer back to it and move things along to the next stage.

10 Size up your customer

In business-to-business selling, the vast majority of customers will fall into one of two broad categories: 'purchase maximizers' or 'purchase satisficers'.

A purchase maximizer is the kind of customer who is always aiming to get as near as is humanly possible to making a 'perfect' purchase. As such, these types of customers will typically hold a full-time buying position with a job title that reflects this responsibility, such as 'Chief Buyer', 'Purchasing Officer' or 'Procurement Manager'. A purchase satisficer, on the other hand, is a very different animal. As the term implies, this kind of customer is only really aiming to make a purchase that's good enough (will *suffice* to *satisfy* their requirements). As long as a product or service is going to do a good job in serving its purpose, they're happy. These types of customers will usually have only an occasional responsibility for buying because it's just something else they do as and when required, alongside their everyday responsibilities. As such, purchase satisficers will typically hold a senior position within their company with a job title such as 'Managing Director', 'Company Director' or 'Owner-Manager'.

Figure A encapsulates the very essence of the differences between the buying styles of these two customer types. A purchase maximizer will spend more time researching their options and deliberating over their decision. They'll place a higher priority on facts and figures and on using a rigorous, systematic decision-making process. They'll tend to be more measured, quietly spoken and analytical. By contrast, a purchase satisficer will spend less time collecting information. They'll quickly make up their minds, relying more on trusting their instincts and sense of judgement than anything else. They'll tend to be more talkative, forceful and opinionated.

Figure A: Customer buying styles

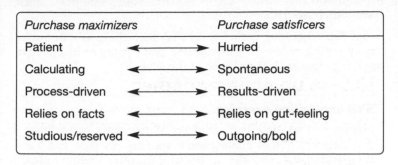

Purchase maximizers		Purchase satisficers
Patient	←——→	Hurried
Calculating	←——→	Spontaneous
Process-driven	←——→	Results-driven
Relies on facts	←——→	Relies on gut-feeling
Studious/reserved	←——→	Outgoing/bold

Clearly, these two types of customer have completely different buying styles, so in order to be able to sell to each type effectively you're going to have to size up your customer and adapt your selling style accordingly, as shown in Figure B.

Figure B: Appropriate selling styles

Purchase maximizers		Purchase satisficers
Be moderately paced	←——→	Be faster paced
Be logical/methodical	←——→	Be inspired/passionate
Stress pros and cons	←——→	Stress pros only
Give full details	←——→	Give highlights only
Acknowledge customer's expertise	←——→	Acknowledge customer's status

For a purchase maximizer, you should aim to come across as the kind of salesperson who is 'the controlled, cool-headed thinker'. This means your manner is going to be rational, deliberate and methodical. Using a calm, moderated speaking voice you're going to deliver a detailed, factual and well-balanced but persuasive sales presentation that clearly acknowledges their technical knowledge and expertise.

By contrast, for a purchase satisficer, you should aim to come across as 'the expressive, quick-witted straightshooter' kind of salesperson. This means your manner is going to be more animated, warm and engaging, and using a brisk, matter-of-fact speaking voice, you're going to deliver a no-frills sales presentation that clearly accommodates your customer's 'must have' purchase goals.

What I'm suggesting is that there's no such thing as a one-size-fits-all selling style – at least not one that's going to be effective anything close to 100 per cent of the time.

Skill acquisition exercise

Prepare and rehearse two variations of your sales presentation that differ in both their content and in your delivery style: one that is tailored to suit purchase maximizers, the other tailored to suit purchase satisficers.

Summary
In this chapter we have looked at how to:

- go through a set-up routine
- project your professionalism
- do the handshake one-two-three-four
- introduce your company as a 'perfect partner'
- build STAR-quality rapport
- qualify your customer
- take control of your selling space
- use an appropriate attention-grabber
- set an agenda
- size up your customer.

02

interviewing-phase selling skills

In this chapter you will learn:
- how to find out all about the customer's specific needs and wants, and uncover the key benefits that they are really looking for.

Opening phase

Set the scene for a businesslike and mutually beneficial conversation to take place between you and the customer.

Interviewing phase

Find out all about the customer's specific needs and wants, and uncover the key benefits that they are really looking for.

Matching phase

Match the customer's needs and wants as closely as possible to the benefits of your product or service offer.

Closing phase

Get the customer's agreement to go ahead, and leave them feeling positive about their purchase decision.

Objection-handling phase

Handle the customer's objection to their complete satisfaction and, if possible, turn it around into a closing opportunity.

11 Ask plenty of open-style questions

If there is one characteristic shared by just about every customer on the planet, it is their need to feel that a salesperson thoroughly understands their purchase situation. Experienced salespeople fully appreciate this and always take their time to interview each customer about every aspect of their individual requirements. They know that the quickest way to kill a sale is to start trying to sell their product or service prematurely, without having first made an effort to really understand their customer's requirements.

It's only by asking open-style questions that you can find out about a customer – what sort of person they are, their needs and wants, hopes and fears, and their vision of the future. To put it another way, it's only by asking open-style questions that you are able to unlock the detailed information you're going to need in order to satisfy a customer and make a sale. In interviewing a customer, there are a number of different open-style questions to employ.

The six 'classic' information-seekers

There are six 'classic' open questions, and the easiest way to remember them is to refer to Rudyard Kipling's famous verse from *The Elephant's Child*:

> **I keep six honest serving-men**
> **(They taught me all I knew);**
> **Their names are What and Why and When**
> **And How and Where and Who.**

So, the six 'classic' open and information-seeking questions are simply those that start with *what, why, when, how, where* or *who,* because they demand a full and expansive answer. Examples include:

- *What are your key buying criteria?*
- *Why is that so important to you?*
- *When will the new factory be completed?*
- *How reliable is your existing system?*
- *Where are you going to relocate your workshop?*
- *Who is involved in operating your machines?*

The 'direct-request' method

This style of open questioning requires that you make a 'direct request' for certain information. The beauty of this method is that it focuses the interview on a specific topic area of your choice. Here are some examples:

- *Tell me more about ...*
- *Describe to me ...*
- *Explain to me ...*
- *Give me an example of ...*

The 'instant-replay' technique

This is when you repeat back to your customer, like an 'instant-replay', a key word or phrase they have just used, but with a quizzical upward inflection in your voice so as to indicate that you would like them to tell you more. For example:

Customer: *I'm concerned about the safety issues ...*

Salesperson: *The safety issues ... ?* (quizzical voice inflection)

The 'fill-in-the-blanks' approach

Using an enquiring tone of voice, this is when you deliberately encourage the customer to 'fill-in-the-blanks' and tell you more about the topic at hand by using the following types of 'tag on' words and phrases to feed off something that's just been said:

- *Which is ... ?*
- *Such as ... ?*
- *And so ... ?*
- *And then ... ?*
- *Because of ... ?*

Although each of the four open-style questioning methods above is powerful in its own right, the real key to effective interviewing is to use a combination of them as necessary. For example, if your customer seems a little timid or reserved, then you need to ask an easy-to-answer 'classic' open question to get them talking more freely. If, on the other hand, he or she has a tendency to ramble, then a 'direct-request' for more information on a specific point will help to keep the conversation focused. If a customer is being a little evasive or unforthcoming on a particular issue, however, then an 'instant-replay' question or a 'fill-in-the-blanks' style of question can be a good way to force their hand and find out what is really on their mind.

Skill acquisition exercise

Using as wide a range of open-style questions as you possibly can, interview a friend or colleague about their favourite hobby or pastime. Continue this exercise until you begin to acquire the habit of using various combinations of open-style questions that draw from them more and more about it, and from every conceivable angle.

---

12 Trigger your customer's imagination

Cast your mind back to the last time you made a major purchase of some kind – perhaps a decision to buy a new home or to go on the holiday of a lifetime. Now ask yourself this: before making your decision, isn't it true that you allowed yourself the luxury of imagining just how good it would feel once you owned that new home or were actually on that holiday? Of course you did! That's why one of the skills of professional selling is an ability to help your customers to engage their own imagination.

You can trigger your customer's imagination simply by asking a question that requires him or her to step out of reality and be creative. Here are three examples showing the types of questions you can ask and the words and phrases you can use:

- *Imagine the perfect xxx machine had been up and running in your factory since the start of the year. Let me ask you, in what ways do you think you'd have benefited from it so far?*

- *Just pretend the perfect xxx service is already in place right now. Tell me, what unnecessary work would it eliminate for you and your staff?*

- *Let's say it's the end of the financial year and with the help of the perfect xxx system you've actually achieved your projected sales target on budget. May I ask, what would that mean to you personally?*

A popular approach is to package your question using the 'Let's assume … What happened …?' format. This is a great technique because it accommodates just about any type of product or service, and once you've asked it, there's only one place your customer can go to come up with an answer: their imagination. Here's how it goes:

> *Let's **assume** you've already owned the perfect **xxxx** for the last 12 months. **What happened** during that 12 month period to convince you it was a good buy?*

In triggering your customer's imagination the key is to ask them to assume ownership of your product or service and to live out the benefits in the theatre of their mind – a place which is full of the possibilities of how good life could be once they've made the decision to buy. The moment your customer starts to imagine a world in which they already own your product or service then you can be sure your job will have instantly become a lot easier.

Skill acquisition exercise

Devise a question that you would feel comfortable asking which would enable you to successfully trigger your customer's imagination. Work out the exact phrasing. Memorize and rehearse it.

---

13 Use closed questions with pinpoint precision

A 'closed question' is a form of question that demands only a one-word answer – usually a 'yes' or a 'no'. As such, it's a very specialized form of question that should always be used with great care during a sales interview. By forcing a customer into giving you only a one-word answer, you are preventing a flowing two-way conversation from taking place. Worse still, the injudicious use of closed questions can easily lead to too many 'nos'. Not that the odd 'no' is necessarily a bad thing, but as a general rule too many 'nos' introduces a disproportionate amount of negativity and this can have the effect of 'freezing you out' of a sale.

Used correctly, however, closed questions can be an extremely effective selling tool. It's just a matter of knowing when and how to use them with pinpoint precision. Let's take a closer look at the two main types of closed question.

The straight closed question

This is the type of closed question that starts with a verb conjugated in the affirmative. Here are some examples:

- *Are you ... ?*
- *Can you ... ?*
- *Could you ... ?*
- *Do you ... ?*
- *Would you ... ?*
- *Have you ... ?*
- *Will you ... ?*
- *Is it ... ?*
- *Does it ... ?*
- *Are there ... ?*

This type of closed question is called 'straight' because it's a totally unbiased and genuine question that simply aims to establish either a 'yes' or a 'no' response. The beauty of asking a few well-chosen straight closed questions is that they can provide you with a lot of factual information in a very efficient and authoritative manner, while at the same time giving you the necessary feedback to be able to steer the subject matter of a conversation in an appropriate direction. Take, for example, the question: 'Do you have any particular colour preferences?' If the customer replies 'no' then you have succeeded in establishing an important fact, enabling you to refocus and direct your next question to some other aspect of their requirement. If, however, the customer says 'yes', then obviously you will need to immediately follow up with a line of open questions in order to find out exactly what colour(s) he or she prefers, for what reasons, and so on.

The loaded closed question

It's a good idea to get as many 'yes' responses as possible from a customer during the course of a sale presentation, *isn't it?* It works really well to build a sort of 'staircase of agreement' between you, *doesn't it?* In fact, I'm building one now, *aren't I?* What's more, you can see exactly how I'm doing it, *can't you?* I'm making a positive statement and then seeking to wrap up your agreement by tagging on to the end of it a verb conjugated in the negative. Otherwise known as the 'wrap-up' technique, this is a classic method of asking a loaded closed question.

However, I could have sought to wrap up your agreement just as easily by putting the verb at the beginning of each statement instead of at the end. I could have said: *Isn't it* a good idea to get as many 'yes' responses as possible from a customer? or *Doesn't it* work really well to build a sort of 'staircase of agreement' between you?

Examples of loaded closed questions include:

Aren't you ... ?	or	*... aren't you?*
Can't you ... ?	or	*... can't you?*
Couldn't you ...?	or	*... couldn't you?*
Don't you ... ?	or	*... don't you?*
Wouldn't you ... ?	or	*... wouldn't you?*
Haven't you ... ?	or	*... haven't you?*
Won't you ... ?	or	*... won't you?*
Isn't it ... ?	or	*... isn't it?*
Doesn't it ... ?	or	*... doesn't it?*
Aren't there ... ?	or	*... aren't there?*

This type of closed question is 'loaded' because it is deliberately designed to elicit a 'yes' response. So, they're a great way to cement the customer's agreement to minor points as you go through the interviewing phase of your sales presentation and beyond. However, don't be too trigger-happy in using them. They may come across as somewhat manipulative and controlling in nature, which means they can very easily irritate the customer. One loaded closed question too many at the wrong time and the whole tone of a conversation may quickly turn from being warm and co-operative to very cold and confrontational. The trick is to use them sparingly and, most importantly, only ever at those times when you can sense sufficient positive stimuli coming back from the customer to feel confident that he or she is likely to respond with genuine agreement.

Skill acquisition exercise

Decide upon the exact wording of a number of (a) straight closed questions, and (b) loaded closed questions that you could usefully employ during the interviewing phase of your sales presentation.

14 Employ the SPOTS interviewing framework

Just as a chat show host on radio or TV needs to have prepared a list of meaningful questions to ask their guest before 'going live', so it is for you as a salesperson. There is no substitute for a well-prepared, well-structured interview with a line of questioning that starts off with a few general questions and then follows up with more searching 'piggybacked' questions that feed off the answers given and become increasingly focused on your customer's particular buying situation.

One way of planning the scope and sequencing of your questions is to employ the SPOTS interviewing framework. SPOTS stands for:

- Situation
- Problem
- Opportunity
- Threat
- Summary.

The idea is to develop a number of key questions in each area before moving on to the next.

S = Situation

Situation questions enable you to gain a thorough understanding of all relevant background information relating to the customer's current situation. For example:

What quality control systems do you use at the moment?

P = Problem

Problem questions enable you to identify any worries, problems, difficulties or 'pain' the customer is experiencing. For example:

How well is your current system performing?

O = Opportunity

Opportunity questions enable you to find out what the customer's ideal situation would be and how he or she would benefit from solving their problem. For example:

What level of improvement do you see as being achievable?

T = Threat

Threat questions enable you to explore the downstream consequences and implications of the customer continuing on their current path without taking any action whatsoever. For example:

How will quality control affect your company's ability to compete in your new export markets?

S = Summary

Summary questions enable you to gain the customer's agreement to your understanding of their needs and wants, and benefits sought. For example:

So as I understand it, what you need is xxx in order that you can xxx Have I got that right?

Make no mistake about it, the sequencing, quality and relevance of your questions will always reveal to the customer your level of experience and expertise as a sales professional in your industry.

Skill acquisition exercise

Using the SPOTS framework, brainstorm with one or more of your colleagues or friends to develop a sequence of questions that will encourage your customers to talk freely and tell you all about their requirements.

15 Mirror the customer's 'personal vocabulary'

Most of us use a vocabulary of about 2,500 words in our everyday conversations. Although we think of the vast majority of these words as being nothing more than 'just a word', a few become especially significant to us. Certain words and phrases take on a special significance because at some point in our lives, and for some good reason, they have become associated with a particular emotion, and that association has become ingrained. While these words and phrases are not necessarily special to anyone else, they are to us. In short, the importance we attach to these words and phrases helps to define us as the unique individuals that we are.

In the world of professional selling, any words or phrases that seem to hold a special significance for a customer are referred to as their 'personal vocabulary'. It's a sort of language-within-a-language that you should tune in to with every new customer. The more you can pick up on it and start to talk the customer's language, the more you'll be enhancing the quality of your interpersonal communications. Your customers will feel as though you better appreciate and understand them and you'll experience a greater sense of customer rapport.

There are three main types of personal vocabulary to pick up on and 'mirror' back to a customer as your sales presentation unfolds:

- 'pet' words
- favourite sayings
- industry buzz-words and jargon.

So that you can be sure of exactly what I'm talking about, let's consider a few examples of each type:

'Pet' words

Most customers have at least one or two favourite words. Typically, they're easily recognizable if for no other reason than how often we hear a customer use them! However, another tell-tale sign is that they're often slightly unusual words. Here's an example:

Example

I had been with a prospective customer for just a few minutes when it became apparent that one of his pet words was 'acknowledge'. He wanted to 'acknowledge' the fact that his business was losing market share and to 'acknowledge' that the time had come to hire-in some marketing expertise. Having picked up on his pet word, I was then able to use it myself on a number of occasions during our conversation. In particular, when I got around to summing up the customer's needs I was able to say 'you acknowledge that ...'

Sometimes, a customer's pet word isn't a real word at all but one that he or she has made up. In these cases don't correct or question your customer's use of this word. As long as the meaning behind the word is entirely understandable then there's no reason why you shouldn't use it yourself. For example:

Example

Steve sells specialist computer systems to retailers. He once told me the story of a customer who said he wanted to 'electronify' his stock control records. Steve knew that what the retailer really meant was to 'computerize' his stock control system, but wisely chose to use the customer's made-up word from that point onwards in his sales presentation.

Favourite sayings

If you notice that a customer is particularly fond of a certain saying, such as 'time flies', or 'as sure as night follows day', then use these terms yourself as the sale progresses. In fact, because sayings often carry a message of universal truth, they can be especially useful as a sales tool – made all the more powerful because you can be sure your choice of language will resonate loud and clear with your customer. For example:

Example

When Mary noticed that her customer's favourite saying was 'there's no time like the present' she was able to replay it back to the customer when the time came to ask for the sale:

As you said yourself, Jeff, there's no time like the present. So, can I write up your order?

Industry buzz-words and jargon

Every industry has its own buzz-words and jargon. For example, in the advertising industry people talk about 'advertorials', 'advergaming', 'psychographics' and 'IMCs', to mention but a few. This type of language signifies that the person using it is an industry 'insider' with special knowledge. For this reason, some salespeople believe they should use a lot of these words. Certainly, they should be familiar with them. However, more often than not a salesperson's gratuitous use of this kind of lingo has a negative effect on a customer because it is seen merely as an attempt to impress. That's why the best time to use a particular buzz-word or piece of industry jargon is when you notice your customer is in the habit of using it as part of their own 'personal vocabulary'. When you observe this simple rule, it becomes a rapport-maker instead of a rapport-breaker.

Skill acquisition exercise

Listen to a local radio 'talkback' show. Focus your attention on becoming aware of the personal vocabulary used by those people who phone in to the programme. Evaluate the ability of the host to make use of this vocabulary as a means of developing a sense of rapport.

16 Signal your questions

Have you ever noticed how the top current affairs journalists and other professional interviewers on radio or TV have a tendency to 'signal' their questions immediately prior to asking them? For example, they commonly use the most basic form of signalling, which is simply to indicate that they are about to ask a question by using a phrase such as:

- *Let me ask you ...*
- *Tell me ...*
- *My next question is ...*
- *I'd like to ask you ...*
- *Another question is ...*
- *May I ask you ...*

Alternatively, they may signal their questions by telling their interviewee what topic they are going to ask about next. For example:

- *Let's turn now to the question of globalization ...*

Sometimes they signal a question by alerting their interviewee to the advantage of answering a particular question by saying something like this:

- *I want to give you the opportunity to publicly state your position on this issue ...*

Similarly, they might signal a question by referring to its importance. For example:

- *One question that's of immense public interest at the moment is ...*

When a particular question is right at the heart of the matter, then as a means of adding further emphasis you'll often hear a professional interviewer double-signal or even triple-signal a question. In other words, they might use a combination of two or three different signals in their build-up to asking a certain question. Here's an example of a double and then a triple-signalled question:

- *Let me ask you* [first signal] *one question that's of immense public interest at the moment* [second signal] *...*
- *Let's turn now to the question of globalization* [first signal]. *I want to give you the opportunity to publicly state your position on this issue* [second signal]; *tell me* [third signal] *...*

As a professional salesperson, you should do exactly the same when interviewing a customer about their needs and wants, and for good reason. Signalling provides your customer with a sense of context and helps them to focus on the question at hand. It also serves as a 'signpost' to lead your customer smoothly through the interviewing phase of your sales presentation, promoting a crystal clear exchange of information. As long as you don't dilute its effects by over-using any one phrase, you'll soon discover signalling can be an effective communication tool that gives you a greater degree of authority during your sales interviews.

Skill acquisition exercise

Identify all the key topics that you cover during the course of your sales interviews. Determine the exact words you could use to signal your intention to question your customers in each of these areas.

---

17 Communicate your empathy

Empathy is the ability to 'put yourself in someone else's shoes' and to be able to see things from their point of view in a considerate and caring way. Clearly, in questioning a customer about their needs and wants, it is essential that you are able to empathize with their buying situation. This is especially important whenever a topic arises that is sensitive or emotional in nature. Not only does it make the customer feel more 'connected' to you on a personal level, but even more importantly, it helps to build their trust and confidence in you as an experienced and professional salesperson.

As you read these words I'm sure that you are already analyzing your own ability to empathize. No doubt you are concluding that you do it most of the time and that you have all the requisite customer knowledge, care and concern to do it rather well. However, let me ask you: *Is your customer always aware that you are truly empathizing with their situation?* My point is that unless you are *communicating* your empathy, unfortunately it will probably be lost on the customer! So here's a simple formula by which you can be sure that you're effectively communicating your empathy. I call it the 'triple A' method:

The first 'A' = Anticipate it

Whenever you are about to ask a question about a sensitive issue, or one that, for some reason, you anticipate is going to necessitate that you communicate empathy, you should signal your concern in the way you set up the question. For example, you could say:

John, I'm very conscious that this is a particularly sensitive subject for you at the moment, however, I do have to ask you ...

The second 'A' = Acknowledge it

When a customer does you the courtesy of answering your question, it is vitally important that you convey to that customer that you are hearing what they are telling you about their feelings. Often the simple act of acknowledgement 'connects' with the customer and has the effect of encouraging him or her to tell you more. You can do this just by nodding slowly and thoughtfully, and by saying:

I hear what you're saying, John.

The third 'A' = Appreciate it

Always thank the customer for sharing their thoughts and telling you about their situation. Once you have done this, but only if you are genuinely able to relate to it, then by all means go on to express the full extent of your understanding and concern for their situation by saying something supportive such as:

Thanks for being candid with me about that John, I can certainly understand how it must make life very difficult for you because ...

Feeling empathy for a customer is one thing but actually showing it is quite another. The 'triple A' formula is a useful way to show a customer that you have the necessary experience and knowledge to be able to relate to their buying situation with forethought, care and consideration.

Skill acquisition exercise

For all those aspects of a typical customer's buying situation that are likely to be sensitive or emotional in some way, role-play your use of the 'triple A' formula with a colleague or friend.

18 Listen actively

The flip-side of asking questions is listening to the answers given. In fact, listening actively rather than passively (showing that you are listening rather than giving a deadpan response) is every bit as important as asking questions.

Being an active listener means making the effort to show that you are comprehending and interested in what is being said. This is a basic skill all salespeople should master because when customers are talking about themselves and their business, to them it's the most important subject under the sun. Active listening demonstrates concern, builds trust and helps reduce any 'sales resistance'. Moreover, it turns you into a brilliant conversationalist. After all, it's often said that people who want to talk about themselves are boring, but people who want to talk about me are brilliant conversationalists!

You can become an expert 'active listener' by acquiring the habit of using the following techniques to show the customer you are listening carefully:

Provide plenty of brief verbal feedback

Use small utterances that encourage the customer to keep on talking but without interrupting their flow. For example:

- *hmm*
- *ah-ah*
- *huh-huh*
- *I see*
- *oh really*
- *I understand.*

Provide plenty of non-verbal feedback

Use your eyes, face and body language to show the customer you're interested in what's being said. For example, nod, smile, tilt your head, stroke your chin, lean forward and so on.

Periodically paraphrase and restate

Use summary statements and restatements to check your level of understanding and comprehension. For example:

So if I understand correctly, what you're saying is ...

Ask reactive questions

Use thoughtful and reflective open questions to request clarification or further information whenever appropriate. For example:

- *How do you mean, exactly?*
- *Tell me more about that ...*

Before asking a reactive question, a good tip is to count to three silently to yourself. This creates a short pause which indicates to your customer that you have been listening attentively and given due consideration to your next question.

Take notes

Making notes not only helps you to concentrate on what's being said but it also reinforces your role as a problem-solver. However, be sure to ask your customer's permission before taking any notes. For example, you might say:

I have some more questions about that. To ensure I don't miss anything would you mind if I take notes?

Then, subsequently, whenever you want to stop to make some notes you can say:

Thanks, that's most helpful ... just give me a moment and I'll make a note of it.

Finally, remember to listen with your brain at all times – and not just with your ears! In other words, learn to listen to what the customer does not say. For example, listen for hesitations and omissions, or words tinged with sarcasm or insincerity, and try to understand the true meaning behind the actual words being spoken.

Skill acquisition exercise

Paying close attention to your use of each of the techniques described above, practise your active listening skills during a mock needs-analysis interview with a colleague or friend.

19 Read your customer's body language

Face-to-face communication always has two components – the audible and the inaudible. The audible component relates to what people say and the words they use. It is the spoken language of communication. The inaudible component, on the other hand, relates to the unspoken 'silent' messages conveyed through the 'body language' of facial expressions, gestures, eye contact, body posture, hand, arm and leg movements, and so on.

Most experts agree that since the majority of signals communicated through a person's body language happen spontaneously and at a subconscious level, they are likely to be a more accurate representation of what someone is really thinking than what they might actually be telling you verbally. So, being able to read your customer's body language is a vital selling skill. You can use it to get some sense of your customer's underlying mood and to gain greater insight into what they are really thinking. You can also use it to help minimize any ambiguity or misunderstandings and to provide for a greater clarity of information exchange.

It is useful to think of the signals a customer communicates through their body language as being a bit like the signals on a set of traffic lights: there are green ones, amber ones and red ones.

Green signals

These signals indicate that your customer is fully engaged in and responding favourably to your sales presentation. Some classic examples of the main types of green signals to look out for are when your customer is:

- sitting upright or leaning slightly forwards in their chair
- making lots of direct eye contact
- nodding periodically
- looking at you with a relaxed and pleasant facial expression
- stroking their chin in a thoughtful way
- sitting or standing relatively still while talking.

So what should you do when observing 'code green' body language? Well, just keep on doing what you're doing because you're definitely going well and are on the right track!

Amber signals

These signals suggest that your customer is a little unclear about some aspect of the conversation or perhaps a touch bored or even impatient with it. Examples of amber signals to look out for are when your customer:

- begins to slump down in their chair or starts to lean slightly away from you
- blinks rapidly as if they are struggling to maintain mental focus
- has a blank or perplexed facial expression
- is doodling with their pen or fiddling with their bracelet or ring.

So what should you do when observing 'code amber' body language? Well, clearly you need to proceed with great care because you're probably in danger of losing your customer's attention. Depending on the specific situation at hand, it might be appropriate to quickly move the conversation along to a different topic, suggest a stretch break, begin to signal your questions more clearly or to re-double your efforts as an active listener.

Red signals

These signals show that your customer is responding negatively to your sales presentation. They may have lost interest in it or even become disapproving of it. Some examples of red signals to look out for are when your customer:

- shuffles in their chair so that their entire body is tilted away from you
- avoids making eye contact
- has a tense or frowning facial expression
- folds their arms across their chest
- crosses their legs in a direction that's away from you
- clenches their hands or starts to drum their fingers on the desktop.

So what should you do when observing 'code red' body language? Well, you'll certainly need to act quickly and decisively because a total communication breakdown is imminent. This means you have little option but to stop your presentation dead in its tracks and let your customer know that you're well aware that there's a problem. Ask him or her what it is, apologize for anything untoward you might have inadvertently said or done, and do whatever it takes to re-establish rapport before continuing.

Please note that the key to learning to accurately read your customer's body language is to look out for a *pattern* of signals. Be aware that an isolated gesture is probably meaningless. As soon as you notice a number of signals occurring, however, especially when you can see that they are forming a familiar pattern, then it's time to act.

Skill acquisition exercise

Select a TV channel featuring a serious interview. Hit the 'record' button and with the sound turned off try to sharpen your ability to read the body language of both the interviewee and interviewer. Then turn on the sound and replay the interview to see how well you've done.

---

20 Provide information-affirmation

Here's the story of how I learned about this powerful little selling skill:

Example

Many years ago I made an appointment to see a personal financial planner to help sort out my financial affairs. I arrived at his office at the agreed time, and after we had exchanged the usual pleasantries he explained to me that before he could work out a plan he would need to spend our first meeting interviewing me in some depth in order to gain a thorough understanding of my life situation, financial priorities and so on. Consequently, he began to fire away with a seemingly endless barrage of increasingly detailed and very personal questions. At first I didn't mind answering his questions. After all, it was in my interests to help him do his job. However, as time wore on, the intensity of his questioning and the feeling of being under a microscope started to take its toll on my patience and motivation levels. I even began to resent what seemed, at times, to be an almost gratuitous intrusion into some of the most private areas of my life. So, after being on the receiving end of almost a full hour of relentless questioning, it was with great relief that the interview finally came to an end. Driving away from his office, I felt both exhausted and more than a little irritated. However, as I had a professional interest in the interviewing process itself, I reflected on our meeting and tried to make sense of my negative reaction to his technique. It certainly wasn't that the guy was a bad interviewer; in fact he'd been a great listener, had taken copious notes and had 'signalled' most of his questions. But something had been missing and, infuriatingly, I just couldn't put my finger on it.

A few months later when I was recounting my story to a friend, the penny finally dropped. There was one key skill, one facet of the financial planner's interviewing style, that was lacking that day. A skill that I've since realized is fundamental to any in-depth sales interview because it helps to keep a customer interested and motivated to answer questions: during a lengthy sales interview, you owe it to your customer to provide him or her with frequent 'information-affirmation', i.e. plenty of positive feedback about the value of the information you are being given.

It seems so obvious, doesn't it? But I am convinced that most salespeople routinely fail to appreciate the importance of providing their customers with this kind of feedback.

There are two types of information-affirmation that you can feed back to your customers – simple and complex. During the course of an interview you should aim to provide your customer with an appropriate and varied mix of both types.

Simple information-affirmation

Simple information-affirmations involve using a few stock phrases to acknowledge the value of the information you're receiving, such as:

- *Thanks, that's very interesting.*
- *Thanks, that's most helpful.*
- *Thanks, that's really useful.*
- *Thanks, that's extremely valuable.*

Complex information-affirmation

A complex information-affirmation is used more sparingly. It goes one step further than a simple information-affirmation in that it requires that you go on to give your customer a specific explanation or reason as to *why* you think their information is 'interesting', 'helpful', 'useful' or 'valuable'. You can turn a simple information-affirmation into a complex one just by adding the word 'because' and then filling in the blanks, like this:

- *Thanks, that's very useful, because ...*
- *Thanks, that's most helpful, because ...*
- *Thanks, that's really useful, because ...*
- *Thanks, that's extremely valuable, because ...*

At this point, if you're thinking to yourself 'that's all very well, but often my customers don't give me the quality of information I need', then please remember that poor information quality is not your customer's fault; it's your fault for not asking the right questions in the first place! To put it another way, as a professional salesperson it's your responsibility to ensure that you get the quality of information you need – and when you do you should always take the time to affirm it with gratitude, sincerity and enthusiasm.

Skill acquisition exercise

Make a list of all the key pieces of detailed information you typically receive from a customer. Next, adjacent to each item, write either a simple or complex information-affirmation that you would feel comfortable feeding back to your customers. Memorize and practise your information-affirmations.

---

21 Keep control of the interview

With some customers it's all too easy to find yourself losing control of the sale almost before you've had a chance to get started! I'm talking about the ones who just don't seem to want to be questioned about their needs and wants and instead seem determined to turn the tables on you by becoming your interview*er* rather than interview*ee*. As a young salesperson I can still remember dreading the thought of coming across these customers because I felt powerless to stop them from totally dominating the conversation, undermining my confidence and compromising my chances of making a sale. Then one day, quite by chance, I discovered the secret of controlling a sales interview. Here's what happened:

Example

Picture the scene ... It was a cold Tuesday morning many years ago and I was frantically working away in my garage trying to fix my car in time for an appointment when I caught sight of a door-to-door salesperson knocking on my next-door-neighbour's front door. As I was running late and in a bit of a hurry, it has to be said that the last person I wanted to see was this door-to-door salesperson. Sure enough though, he eventually started walking down my driveway carrying two huge suitcases full of his wares. So, in an effort to get rid of him as quickly as possible, I kicked open the garage door and shouted in my roughest and most aggressive-sounding tone of voice: 'What are you selling?' to which, with a twinkle in his eye and an extra spring in his step, he replied: 'What do you want?' Now as it happened, at that precise moment what I really wanted was a certain type of screwdriver to enable me to undo a particularly obstinate engine screw, and needless to say, he was able to sell one to me! Later on that morning as I drove to my appointment I reflected on his technique. I realized that by answering my question with a question he'd been able to sidestep almost certain rejection while at the same time putting himself in total control of the sale, and to my ultimate benefit. What a brilliant piece of selling!

Let's review the lessons I learned from that door-to-door salesperson. The first lesson is to understand that when two people are having a conversation, it's the person asking the questions who's actually in control of the subject matter of that conversation and *not* the one who's doing all the talking. The second lesson is to appreciate that the moment you find yourself beginning to lose control of a sales interview, you must immediately seize back the initiative by answering their question with a question. You should even be prepared to 'question wrestle' with your customer if that's what it takes. Yes, learning to execute this technique will feel a little uncomfortable (and even impolite) at first but it can and must be done, because the more a customer pushes you into assuming the role of an interviewee, the harder it becomes to re-establish an appropriate level of authority over the sale as the interviewer. Please note, however, that there is plenty of scope for delivering this technique with varying degrees of subtlety. If needs be, it can be softened considerably by adopting a friendly manner and providing your customer with a brief answer to their question prior to asking one back. For example, in computer store:

Customer: *What sort of printers do you have in stock?*

Salesperson: *Well, we have an extremely wide range, Madam* [big smile] *... tell me, what sort of printing do you want to be able to do?*

A third and final lesson is to realize that you won't be doing your customers any favours by allowing them to control your sales conversations. Look at it like this: if you haven't been able to find out all about their buying requirements, your customer is being deprived of the opportunity to take advantage of all your knowledge, experience and expertise in helping him or her to make the best possible purchase decision.

Skill acquisition exercise

Recall a previous sales conversation when you lost control by readily answering too many of the customer's questions. Now imagine yourself in the same situation in the future. What could you say to prevent this from happening again?

Summary

In this chapter we have looked at how to:

- ask plenty of open-style questions
- trigger your customer's imagination
- use closed questions with pinpoint precision
- employ the SPOTS interviewing framework
- mirror the customer's 'personal vocabulary'
- signal your questions
- communicate your empathy
- listen actively
- read your customer's body language
- provide information-affirmation
- keep control of the interview.

03 matching-phase selling skills

In this chapter you will learn:
- how to match the customer's needs and wants as closely as possible to the benefits of your product or service offer.

Opening phase

Set the scene for a businesslike and mutually beneficial conversation to take place between you and the customer.

Interviewing phase

Find out all about the customer's specific needs and wants, and uncover the key benefits that they are really looking for.

Matching phase

Match the customer's needs and wants as closely as possible to the benefits of your product or service offer.

Closing phase

Get the customer's agreement to go ahead, and leave them feeling positive about their purchase decision.

Objection-handling phase

Handle the customer's objection to their complete satisfaction and, if possible, turn it around into a closing opportunity.

22 Apply the SELL formula

If there's one phrase that all salespeople should commit to memory it's got to be the three Bs: **Buyers Buy Benefits.**

As a professional salesperson you don't sell the *features* of your product or service, you sell the *benefits* that those features represent to the customer. Most customers' benefits relate to one or more of the following areas:

- saving money
- making money
- saving time
- reducing effort
- obtaining peace of mind
- satisfying an ego
- experiencing sensory pleasure
- improving health
- exercising a social conscience
- achieving personal growth.

So, whereas the term 'features' refers to the characteristics of your product or service, such as its level of quality or its technical configuration, the term 'benefits' refers to what the product or service can do for your customer. To put it another way, whereas a 'feature' answers the customer's question, 'What is it?', a 'benefit' answers the customer's question, 'What's in it for me?' However, effective benefit selling does not mean that you emphasize the benefits of your product or service to the exclusion of mentioning features at all! In fact, describing selected features is important because they provide the means by which you can convince the customer that your product or service is indeed capable of delivering the particular benefits that they are looking for. That's why an ability to link a feature to a benefit lies at the very heart of effective benefit selling. Using the acronym SELL, let's look at how to do it.

S = Show your customer a relevant product or service feature

Draw your customer's attention to a specific feature that you know will enable them to experience a particular benefit from owning or using your product or service, and one that will be well matched to their requirements. For example, the telephone system salesperson might say:

Take a look at this feature, Jim ... it's called a multiaxis facility ...

E = Explain the feature in full detail

Aim to enhance your customer's understanding of the feature by explaining, in detail, how it works, how it can be used, and especially what it does – its advantages/performance characteristics. To continue our example:

It's a computer chip that automatically routes international calls down the cheapest available telephone line ...

L = Link

Use a simple link phrase such as 'and what this means for you is ...' or its equivalent. To continue our example:

... which means that ...

L = Lay out the benefit to the customer

Go beyond a generic, one-size-fits-all approach and spell out the benefit in a way that it makes it as relevant and as meaningful as possible for your customer. To continue our example:

... based on your current calling profile, you'll save around 27 per cent off your monthly phone bill ... and that's about £280 less than you're paying at the moment.

As this example clearly shows, the use of a 'link phrase' is fundamental to being able to sell benefits because it forces you to go on to interpret exactly how a particular feature will benefit your customer. To put it another way, it provides the necessary underlying rationale to ensure that each of your selling points will really make sense and sound credible and attainable to your customers.

> **Skill acquisition exercise**
>
> Make a list of all the features that describe your product or service. Then take each feature on your list and write down the benefit that it represents from the customer's point of view. Next, apply the SELL formula to work out the exact phrasing you're going to use to sell each feature and benefit as effectively as possible. Memorize and rehearse.

23 Sell matching benefits

There are two sorts of salespeople: 'feature creatures' and 'benefit beasties'. Let me explain exactly what I mean by telling you about the day I went shopping for a DVD player to replace my old video cassette player. All I wanted was a basic model that would be very easy to operate and compatible with my existing TV set. Here's what happened:

> **Example**
>
> In the first store I visited, the salesperson was a classic 'feature creature' – the sort who thinks their job is to sell products rather than to help their customers to buy benefits. As soon as I'd expressed an interest in buying a DVD player, I was shown a particular model and was assured that it was the 'best value buy' in the store because it had a whole raft of technical features for doing this, that and the other. However, as each feature was being pointed out at breakneck speed and in excruciating technical detail, I found myself becoming increasingly inattentive and losing interest. There was no way I would use all those features, and in any case I was sure it would be far too complicated to operate. So, at the earliest opportunity I made my excuses, said goodbye and was glad to make a speedy getaway.
>
> Five minutes later I was in a different store across the street. Once again I expressed an interest in buying a DVD player but this time the salesperson was a 'benefit beastie' and her response was very different. She started out by asking me a range of questions to find out how much I knew about DVD players, the type of TV set I had at home, how often I would be using it and so on. Eventually she recommended a particular model and took the time to carefully explain two or three of its main features and benefits that were well matched to my requirements. When I mentioned it seemed to meet my needs perfectly, she promptly closed the sale. Another satisfied customer!

Well, I'm sure my story has a familiar ring to it! It certainly serves to remind us that customers are not interested in buying the features of a product or service. They are only interested in buying benefits – such as obtaining peace of mind, saving time, and so on. Most importantly, however, my story also reminds us that successful selling is NOT about selling the same benefits to all customers all of the time. Rather, the key is to focus on selling *matching* benefits, because the same product or service will almost always benefit different customers in different ways, depending on their individual circumstances. What makes your product or service superior to another is not the fact that it has more features, and consequently more benefits, but that it does more of what a particular customer wants it to do. In a competitive market, if you want to 'snatch' more than your fair share of all those customers out there then you will have to become a 'benefit beastie' and match more customers. It's that simple.

Skill acquisition exercise

Spend a few moments every day repeating the following affirmation to yourself, until it becomes your personal mantra for successful selling:

If I'm going to snatch 'em, I've gotta match 'em!

---

24 Demonstrate your benefits

The ancient Chinese philosopher Confucius is reputed to have said:

> **Tell me and I'll forget**
> **Show me and I'll remember**
> **Involve me and I'll understand**

We all relate to the world through the five senses of sight, sound, touch, smell and taste – and that includes our customers! Consequently, if you can demonstrate the benefits of your product or service in a way that stimulates as many as possible of your customer's five senses, the more they will experience a sense of involvement in the purchase process and the more appealing your product or service is likely to become. Anyone who has ever experienced buying a new car from their local dealership will know exactly what I'm talking about. The sheer thrill of sitting in the driving seat for the first time and then going for a test-drive is what makes the purchase process so enjoyable and the thought of owning the new car so irresistible.

Regardless of what you sell, there's usually a way to demonstrate at least one or two key benefits through harnessing the power of customer involvement. All it takes is some imagination and creative thought. Here are three examples to get you thinking:

- The marine equipment salesperson demonstrates the unique benefit of a new battery-powered navigation device by insisting that their customer drops it over the side of their yacht! After a couple of seconds it bobs back up to the surface and floats. The salesperson then retrieves the device from the water with a small net before handing it over to the customer to inspect it. Amazingly, it hasn't let in water and continues to operate normally.
- The water-softening-equipment salesperson demonstrates the soap cost savings of dishwashing in soft water to a hotel owner by issuing a challenge. Two test tubes are filled half full: one with the hard water straight from the tap in the hotel kitchen and the other with treated tap water. One droplet of liquid soap is then dispensed into each test tube and the hotel owner is asked to vigorously shake the contents of each one until an equal head of lather is achieved in both test tubes. Whereas a single shake is enough to produce an overflowing head of suds in the test tube containing the soft water; no amount of agitation has any effect whatsoever on the hard water in the other test tube.
- The financial services salesperson demonstrates the projected profits of a new savings plan by inviting the customer to enter their investment details into a laptop computer, and then to sit back and watch the year-on-year interest figures appear on screen.

In planning a demonstration, you can maximize its effectiveness by paying close attention to the following points:

1 Before you begin the demonstration, create a little anticipation and intrigue. Tell the customer what is about to happen, what you want them to do, and why.
2 Set the 'stage'. Clear away and keep out of sight anything that could possibly distract the customer from focusing exclusively on taking part in your demonstration.

3 Put the customer 'in the driving seat'. In other words, maximize the potential for the customer to be able to taste, smell, touch, see, hear and experience the benefits of using and/or owning your product or service.

4 Encourage your customer to spend as much time as possible getting involved with your demonstration. Make encouraging remarks. Tell them they're 'catching on fast', 'doing well' or whatever is appropriate.

5 During the demonstration, keep the benefits in the spotlight at all times by relating them to your customer's situation.

6 At the conclusion of the demonstration, be sure to summarize all the key points.

Skill acquisition exercise

Design a method of demonstrating one or more of the major benefits of your product or service. Make sure that it will maximize the customer's involvement by appealing to as many of their five senses as possible. Plan how you will carry it out to maximum effect.

---

25 Translate benefits into pounds and pence

Just because you tell a customer that a particular feature of your product or service means that they will be able to benefit by 'increasing their sales', 'reducing their costs' (or whatever) it does NOT mean you've done your job as a salesperson. You see, the problem with this sort of 'benefit telling' is that it's just too generalized. It ignores the fact that every business customer views their circumstances as unique and that what he or she really wants to know, specifically and in financial terms, is by *how much* you can help to increase their sales or reduce their costs and by *how much* your offer is more cost-effective relative to their alternatives. The point is, 'benefit telling' often amounts to little more than parrot-fashion selling because it requires very little effort and usually means that the salesperson has failed to 'go to work' for the customer. By contrast, 'benefit selling' means that you go one step further and really spell out the full value to the customer of each benefit and that you do so in specific and measurable financial terms relative to their individual business situation. In the end, you've simply got to get down to the nitty-gritty of translating benefits into pounds and pence. It's what business-to-business selling is all about.

Clearly, some types of benefits more readily lend themselves to being translated into financial terms (such as increasing sales or reducing costs), whereas others (such as saving time or obtaining peace of mind) aren't quite so easy to convert. Nonetheless, even in the difficult cases I'd strongly encourage you to rise to the challenge. Through adopting a customer perspective and a little creative thinking, you'll almost always be able to find a way. Here's a good example:

Example

Time saving is a major benefit of the stock control software packages that Jeremy sells to retail owner-managers. Here's his take on benefit selling: 'At a certain point in my sales presentation I ask my customers to write down a ballpark figure of their net annual earnings. I then ask them to divide it by their estimate of the total number of hours they work during a year in order to work out an approximation of their hourly rate. Once people can see exactly how much their time is worth to them, it's amazing how quickly they get serious about wanting to free up some of their valuable time so that it can be spent more productively in other areas of the business ... and it's my job to talk them through exactly that.'

Helping a customer to measure the financial value of your proposition usually means that you will have to work closely with them to go through every aspect of their cost–benefit equation. This is an exacting process that demands a great deal of skill, experience, expertise and judgement. However, it is well worth the effort. Make no mistake about it, this is the highest level of service a salesperson can perform for a customer and when it's done in a professional manner it is always appreciated. After all, how else can your customer be expected to make a fully informed purchase decision?

Skill acquisition exercise

Brainstorm with your colleagues or friends to work out the best way to translate each of the main benefits of your product or service into a financial value for the customer.

---

26 Substantiate your claims

No matter how well you explain a benefit, your assertion alone is not necessarily going to be proof enough for the customer. To put it another way, customers are often sceptical about the claims salespeople make and either consciously or subconsciously they are likely to be questioning the validity of your proposition. So you should always be ready to support your case by providing the customer with as much proof as possible. For this purpose you should carry a sales presentation folder and/or laptop computer files containing at least some of the following sales aids.

Photographs

Some of the best photographs to show a customer are:

- 'amazing but true' photographic evidence of a dramatic demonstration taking place
- a pair of 'before' and 'after' photographs presented side by side
- a sequence of photographs that show the methods and processes involved in making your product or carrying out your service
- close-ups showing the detail of some aspect of your product or the materials from which it is made
- a series of 'in action' shots showing the different situations and places where your product is being used.

Illustrative drawings

Illustrative drawings or artist's impressions are invaluable if you are selling a design service or a product that is still at the concept stage. For example, a real estate salesperson would typically use an artist's impression of a planned residential development to great effect as a way of communicating key features and benefits to a prospective home owner.

Technical drawings

Technical drawings can be particularly useful when you want to explain certain aspects of your product. For example, a black and white line-drawing or a 3D computer graphic would be ideal for showing your customer the details of a specific feature and benefit associated with the internal mechanics of a new type of fork-lift truck.

Cartoons

A cartoon strip or storyboard can be a superb way to explain a sequence of events, especially if there is an element of education involved. For example, a salesperson I know sells an ingenious mobile display stand by referring to a cartoon strip as a means of showing how easy it is to unpack, erect and then dismantle again, and all within a 20-minute timeframe.

Video clips

Moving pictures with a soundtrack can be an extremely useful way of substantiating your claims, especially when, for logistical or safety reasons, you are unable to demonstrate them 'live'. For example, a bullet-proof-vest salesperson I know shows dramatic footage of his CEO shooting himself in the stomach as a means of demonstrating the effectiveness of his product!

Letters of recommendation or thanks

A signed letter of recommendation or a thank-you letter from a satisfied customer is a brilliant sales aid, especially when it's the original copy written on their company notepaper.

Published articles and reports

If a journalist has ever 'road-tested' your product or service, or written any type of feature article or report in which he or she has independently assessed your product or service and made some favourable remarks about it, then of course this represents an invaluable source of proof relating to the features and benefits of your offer.

Research data

For products or services that are technical or scientific in nature, then the provision of hard evidence in the form of research-based data can be especially convincing, particularly if it has been independently certified by someone in a position of authority, such as a doctor or a university professor.

Customer lists

The old adage that 'hundreds of customers can't be wrong' is still a powerful argument that carries a lot of weight with prospective customers.

One way to draw your customers' attention to the above sales aids is to simply 'show and tell' (i.e. show it to them and then tell them about it). However, whenever possible, the best way is to ask an involvement question first, *before* you show and tell. To illustrate what I mean, let's take the example of a salesperson selling a new type of industrial wastewater purification system. When the time comes for the salesperson to substantiate the claim that this system is capable of dramatically improving the purity of a particular customer's wastewater, the conversation unfolds like this:

> Salesperson: *As a matter of fact, we've just had the system independently tested by Professor Jones and his team at City University. Tell me, just out of curiosity, what would be your guess of the best possible percentage output of water purity achievable for the throughput levels you're talking about?* (Asks)
>
> Customer: *Oh, I don't know, maybe about 90 per cent.*
>
> Salesperson: *Well, take a look at the data for yourself.* (Shows) *It shows that with our new system, water purity is recorded at an incredible 97 per cent!* (Tells)

Make no mistake about it, every time you substantiate your claims with proof and evidence, you'll be magnifying your credibility in the eyes of the customer. Pure dynamite!

Skill acquisition exercise

Assemble a range of sales aids that will enable you to prove, as far as possible, each of your benefits to the customer. Decide how you can use each one to maximum effect.

---

27 Master the art of storytelling

Telling a story dramatizes your selling points and makes them more memorable, real and believable. It can also make the buying process a more pleasurable experience for your customers. After all, everyone enjoys a good story. Depending on the situation at hand there are two types of story that can be effective as a selling tool: a success story and a failure story.

A success story

A success story is when you tell a story about a previous customer who, for some particular reason, was extremely glad they bought from you. This is a particularly useful type of story to tell when you need to support your claims about how a customer would benefit from using your product or service. For example, a tractor salesperson could tell the story of a nearby farmer who has been able to save himself more than six hours of work per week since purchasing a certain model – going into detail about exactly how he used the tractor, and, of course, what he does with all his extra spare time!

A failure story

A failure story is when you tell the story of a previous customer who decided not to buy from you and then, for some particular reason, later regretted that decision. This would be an appropriate story to tell if a customer seems uncertain about their level of requirement relative to one or more aspects of your offer. For example, the tractor salesperson could tell the story of another farmer who only six months earlier had decided not to buy and then later on regretted not having the benefit of various features during a particularly wet winter season – going on to explain how it had ended up costing him a great deal of money in lost revenues.

A useful approach to storytelling is the 'feel–felt–found' method because it indicates that, at least to some extent, you are able to relate to your customer's circumstances. With this approach you use the words 'feel–felt–found' as the structure for telling the story. For example:

*I think I know how you **feel** Michael.*

*Mr Smith from the ABC Company **felt** the same way,*

*but once he bought it (or decided not to buy), what he **found** was that ...*

Note that for maximum effectiveness you should always tell the relevant parts of a story in as much detail as you can. Include names and dates and quote as many facts and figures as possible. Above all, remember that a story should always be totally and completely true. Nothing a salesperson can ever say will be more compelling or convincing to a customer than the truth.

Skill acquisition exercise

Identify at least one success story and one failure story that would be useful for you to be able to tell from now on, as and when required.

---

28 Handle your product with pride

Cast your mind back to the last time you went to a jewellery store to buy a necklace or a bracelet. Do you recall how the salesperson carefully handled each piece of jewellery they showed to you as if it were the most precious piece in the world? Well of course this is brilliant salesmanship and for at least two good reasons. Firstly, it inspires great confidence in the expertise and professionalism of the salesperson. After all, surely only someone who is genuinely knowledgeable and enthusiastic about their work would handle their products with such obvious pride – right? Secondly, it serves to enhance the perception of product quality and value in the mind of a customer. Surely only something that is well worth having and paying good money for would be worthy of such reverence and respect – right?

Your customers will be similarly impressed if you handle your product or samples with this kind of pride and appreciation. It doesn't matter if it is an industrial product or one that is 'positioned' at the lower end of a market, because every customer wants to believe in both the salesperson and the value-for-money of their offer. Even if you don't sell a tangible product this principle still applies. If you sell a pure service, for example insurance, then it is more important than ever to handle your company's documentation, brochures and other sales materials with a similar show of respect and pride because, in effect, these resources are your only means of 'showcasing' your offer to the customer.

My research has shown that after a customer has bought an item of jewellery from a top jewellery salesperson, some of the key words that they use to describe how the salesperson handled their product are:

- loving
- caring
- admiring
- expert
- respectful
- mesmerizing
- impassioned
- confident
- knowledgeable
- enthusiastic
- professional.

If your product-handling methods could elicit responses like these from your customers, just think what it might do for your sales figures!

Skill acquisition exercise

Brainstorm with your colleagues or friends to work out the best way to handle your product and/or sales materials in front of the customer. Rehearse your new methods until you feel entirely comfortable using them.

---

29 Use your pen to help you sell well

In the world of politics it's often said that 'the pen is mightier than the sword'. In the world of professional selling this statement is equally true. It may seem a little strange, but your pen is arguably the most useful 'prop' at your disposal. When used properly, there's no doubt that it can help you to sell more persuasively. Take a look at the following examples.

Use your pen as a pointer

Get into the habit of using your pen as a pointer whenever you want the customer's attention focused on a certain aspect of your product or perhaps something in your presentation folder or on screen that is of specific interest. A particularly effective way of doing this is to hold your pen upright in front of your customer's eyes and request that they look directly at the tip of your pen. Once you can see their eyes are trained on the tip, ask them to stay focused on it as you move the pen slowly in the direction of whatever it is you want them to look at more closely. Keep checking that their eyes are still trained on the tip until you eventually bring it to rest, touching the item of interest. At this point your customer's eyes will be focused on exactly what you want them to be looking at! This is a magical little technique that is fun to use and always works well.

Use your pen to illustrate

Whenever possible you should take the opportunity to describe the features and benefits of your product or service by using your pen to draw explanatory illustrations, pictures, sketches or diagrams. This 'chalk and talk' approach helps to keep your presentation fresh, lively and interesting. For example, if a benefit of your product or service is to reduce a customer's staffing by 20 per cent, then you could illustrate this by drawing a pie chart as follows:

Similarly, you could use your pen to help communicate the financial implications or any other relevant calculations. For example:

$$£7,800 \div 52 = £150 \text{ savings per week}$$

Use your pen to help you close

You can use your pen to help close the sale more smoothly and professionally simply by making it available to the customer when the time comes for them to authorize the paperwork. If you don't have a pen ready and waiting at this critical moment then you'll waste a few valuable seconds searching for one – which may be just enough time for your customer to cool off and change their mind! So, at the critical moment, ensure your pen is at hand, either by gently laying it down on the table in front of the customer or alternatively by calmly passing it over with an air of positive expectation. Incidentally, providing the customer does use your pen to authorize their purchase, you might consider giving it to them as a small token of your appreciation or as a souvenir to mark the occasion of their purchase. It's a nice touch, but only if your pen is of good quality, or has some other special novelty value.

Skill acquisition exercise

Think through every step of your sales presentation and ask yourself: in what ways could I use my pen to help me to sell more effectively from now on?

---

30 Power-pack your benefits

Federal Express, the worldwide courier company, has one of my favourite business slogans: Absolutely, positively, overnight.

I like it because it says exactly what a customer wants to hear and in no uncertain terms: I will enjoy the total peace of mind that comes with knowing that no matter where in the world I want to send my package, I can be sure it will be delivered within 24 hours. No ifs, no buts, no maybes. How's that for a power-packed benefit!

Now ask yourself – when you're explaining the benefits of your offer to customers, can you honestly say that you do so in an equally powerful and unequivocal fashion? That is, in a way that doesn't leave a single trace of doubt in their mind as to the depth of your conviction? Well, if you're anything like most salespeople there's probably room for improvement because the nature of benefit selling is such that you're either totally convincing or you're not. If a customer detects even the slightest hint of uncertainty in your communication style then they will almost inevitably seize upon it and respond with a degree of scepticism. The truth is that you simply cannot afford to be anything less than totally convincing in the way you sell a benefit because your hesitation may sow the seeds of doubt in your customer's mind.

You can power-pack your benefits by paying close attention to two interrelated components of your communication style: *what* you say (i.e. the choice of words and phrases you use) and *how* you say it.

Power-pack what you say

With regard to *what* you say, be careful not to fall into the trap of using any words and phrases which could sound even remotely weak or which could be open to misinterpretation. Instead, take a leaf out of Federal Express's book and use only powerful and emotionally-charged words and phrases that will convey an uncompromising belief in the benefits of your offer. For example:

Don't say	Do say
I think …	*I am totally and utterly convinced …*
I have little doubt …	*I have absolutely no doubt …*
I guess …	*I know for sure …*
I'd say …	*I'd strongly recommend …*

Power-pack how you say it

With regard to *how* you should communicate a benefit, once again there can be no room for misinterpretation. Everything about your manner should convey an air of unswerving confidence in what you have to offer as well as a passionate belief in its value to your customer. I'm talking about every aspect of your body language, and especially your tone of voice, your facial expression and the look in your eye. Indeed, the intensity of your conviction should be almost palpable to the customer. If you're going to say it anyway, you might as well say it with every ounce of conviction that you can muster.

Skill acquisition exercise

Practise the words, phrases and body language (gestures, facial expressions etc.) you intend to use that will project your total and unequivocal belief in the value-to-the-customer of your offer.

31 Know when and how to mention the competition

In these days of rapidly increasing competition, we salespeople might be forgiven for being more than a little confused about the wisdom of referring to our competitors during the course of a sales presentation, and especially when it comes to the part when we are explaining the unique benefits of our offer to the customer. The key questions are: 'Should the existence of competitors be acknowledged?' and if so, 'How should we refer to them?' So here are the rules for when and how to mention the competition.

Rule one

If your customer does not mention the competition then neither should you. *Never* discuss the competition in any way unless you have to. Just carry on with your sales presentation as if they do not exist.

Rule two

If your customer mentions the competition in passing, not by naming them specifically but in such a way that it signals to you that he or she is aware of their choices, then you should simply refer to them as 'all the others' or 'all the rest'. Don't give away free advertising for any of your competitors by mentioning their names.

Rule three

If your customer tells you that you are up against a specific competitor, ask the customer to tell you which one before proceeding to acknowledge this competitor as being a good company with a reputable product or service. Then go on to point out the superior benefits to the customer of your offer compared with theirs. Never put your rival company down. Put the focus on selling the superiority of your offer, not the inferiority of theirs.

Rule four

If yours is a relatively small company and the customer mentions that he or she is considering buying from the largest and most well-known company in the market, then feel free to mention the name of this competitor as often as you like because by comparing yourselves with the market leader your company will only gain further credibility. So, acknowledge their status as the market leader but then go on to sell the benefits of buying from a small specialist company like yours: one with greater agility and flexibility to be able to better meet their needs, one that will provide a far more personalized service, and one that has to work harder to prove themselves and to keep their customers satisfied.

Rule five

If during the course of your sales presentation it becomes apparent that due to an unusual set of circumstances your product or service will not satisfy a particular customer's requirements in some fundamental way, then by all means go ahead and recommend a competitor's product that will. You may not win the sale but you will win the customer's respect for being a highly professional salesperson working for a highly professional company. Gold-dust!

Skill acquisition exercise

Commit to memory the five rules outlined above and resolve that from now on you'll apply them to the letter.

---

32 Sell your secret weapon

Guess what? You have a secret weapon! One that is totally under your control and that can provide you with an extra competitive edge whenever you need it. Think about it. Whatever else your competitors might have to offer ... they don't have YOU! They don't have a salesperson with your dedication and commitment to providing customers with the best possible after-sales personal service – someone who is prepared to 'go the extra mile' on their behalf to ensure all goes smoothly. What I'm suggesting is that no matter how well you sell your company's reputation for providing great service, this will not be anything like as convincing as your personal assurances that you yourself will make a special effort to look after them post-sale.

Here's a list of some of the many types of after-sales services that you could consider offering to your customers; services that go over and above the norm for a salesperson to offer, and as such encourage a customer to want to buy from you and not from your competitors:

- Offer to speed up the processing of your customer's order by tracking order status, checking shipping and delivery schedules and so on.
- Offer to personally oversee product installation and set-up, including operator training.
- Offer to liaise between your people and theirs, ensuring good communication, co-ordination, co-operation and collaboration as appropriate.
- Offer to monitor the ongoing performance of your product or service post-sale, relative to your customer's original purchase goals.
- Offer to be available 24/7 as a first point of contact in case of an emergency or urgent requirement of any kind.
- Offer to keep your customer updated regarding any useful new research information, product application techniques and so on.

In offering any of these types of additional services, don't simply tell your customer about them – *sell them!* This can be done by addressing your customer's concerns one-by-one (as necessary) and by asking him or her a specific 'straight' closed question which begins with the words:

> *Tell me, Michael, would it set your mind at rest if I promise to ...*

This is a magical little formula because you can tag onto the end of it any additional service you are prepared to offer that you think would be likely to inspire a greater confidence in buying from you. What's more, it makes it perfectly obvious that what you're offering is something you yourself are prepared to do specifically for that customer.

Showing a customer that you are prepared to go the extra mile can be very compelling. In fact, in a competitive situation, a customer will often be more convinced by the depth of your conviction to serve him or her to the very best of your ability than by anything else. It's a great way to differentiate yourself from the competition, add value, win your customer's confidence and tip the balance of their decision in your favour.

Skill acquisition exercise

Ask yourself this question: 'Over and above my company's standard offer, what additional services could I offer that would be of high value to my customers but would be something I could do at a low or no cost to me?'

Summary

In this chapter we have looked at how to:

- apply the SELL formula
- sell matching benefits
- demonstrate your benefits
- translate benefits into pounds and pence
- substantiate your claims
- master the art of storytelling
- handle your product with pride
- use your pen to help you sell well
- power-pack your benefits
- know when and how to mention the competition
- sell your secret weapon.

04
closing-phase
selling skills

In this chapter you will learn:
- how to get the customer's agreement to go ahead, and leave them feeling positive about their purchase decision.

Opening phase
Set the scene for a businesslike and mutually beneficial conversation to take place between you and the customer.

Interviewing phase
Find out all about the customer's specific needs and wants, and uncover the key benefits that they are really looking for.

Matching phase
Match the customer's needs and wants as closely as possible to the benefits of your product or service offer.

Closing phase
Get the customer's agreement to go ahead, and leave them feeling positive about their purchase decision.

Objection-handling phase
Handle the customer's objection to their complete satisfaction and, if possible, turn it around into a closing opportunity.

33 Tune in to buying signals

Question: When is the right time to ask that closing question?
Answer: When our customer gives us a buying signal. A buying signal is anything a customer says or does which suggests they have an interest in going ahead with making a purchase. Indeed, when people talk about the need for 'good timing' in selling, what they are referring to is the salesperson's ability to recognize and respond appropriately to a buying signal. Since most customers are reluctant to come right out and say 'OK, I'm getting close to making a decision now and I'd like you to help me to make up my mind', it's useful to think of a buying signal as being a sort of coded language for telling you they're interested. Here's a list of some classic examples. It's by no means a definitive listing of all the buying signals you could ever receive but it does give you a flavour of what to look out for. It's a buying signal when the customer:

- exclaims 'It looks perfect!'
- asks 'So how much is it?'
- starts to talk 'past the sale', i.e. as if they already own your product or service
- offers you an additional argument to support your case
- picks up the agreement form to read some of the fine print
- uses a calculator to check the numbers relating to a particularly important element in their decision
- enquires about the potential for modifying a certain product specification
- makes a thoughtful sounding 'hmm …' in response to your discussions on a specific purchase variable.

Notably, some of the buying signals above are stronger than others in that they indicate a greater degree of interest. Perhaps you've already spotted that I've put four stronger ones in the top half of my list and four weaker ones in the bottom half. Nevertheless, during the course of a sales presentation, it is imperative that you're tuned in to watching and listening for any and every type of buying signal because each time you miss one you're throwing away a precious opportunity to ask an appropriate closing question. This is very easily done, especially when you are preoccupied with trying to get your sales points across.

Please also note that many salespeople make the unfortunate mistake of assuming that a buying signal is only ever going to crop up towards the end of their sales presentation. Although this is often the case, it could occur at any time. Your customer might well be getting ready to make their purchase decision sooner than you think!

Finally, if due to the unusual nature of your type of business, you believe you get less than your fair share of buying signals, then please consider this fact: *good salespeople get more buying signals!* I'm afraid there's nowhere to hide. Nine times out of ten, when a customer gives you a buying signal it's actually a reflex response to good selling. In other words, the more successful you become at stimulating the desire to buy, the more buying signals you'll receive.

Skill acquisition exercise

Prepare a comprehensive list of all the various buying signals you might get from customers. Memorize your list so that you will be able to instantly recognize every buying signal that you receive from now on.

---

34 Trial close after a weak buying signal

A trial close is a conditional closing question such as an 'If … then …' or 'Let's just suppose …' type question, and the time to ask it is when you receive your cue from the customer in the form of a weak buying signal. A weak buying signal is anything a customer says or does which suggests a tentative interest in making a purchase. For example, let's say the customer gives you a weak buying signal by expressing a cautious interest in taking advantage of some special finance terms. It comes in the form of a thoughtful sounding 'hmm … ' just after you've explained that your company's finance options mean that longer repayment periods will not necessarily incur higher interest rate charges. Then at this point, you might say:

> *If we could work out a way of extending your repayment period at no extra charge **then** would you be happy to go ahead on that basis?*

or

> *Let's just suppose that we could work out a way of extending your repayment period at no extra charge. Would you consider going ahead on that basis?*

Please bear in mind that sometimes it will be inappropriate to pose a trial closing question in this way. This is because from the customer's point of view there's always a fine line between a trial-closing question that sounds assertive and 'fair' and one that just sounds too controlling and manipulative. Consequently, depending on your reading of the situation you might prefer to soften the delivery of a trial close just to make sure it isn't going to irritate your customer. This can be done by signalling to him or her that you don't wish to offend, immediately prior to asking the question. Here are three examples of the types of phrases that can be used:

- *I don't mean to put you under any pressure; nevertheless, may I ask you ...*
- *It's not my intention to play hardball; nonetheless, please tell me ...*
- *I'm not trying to be pushy; however, let me ask you ...*

The key advantage of a trial-closing question is that a negative response does not lock you out of the sale because it is conditional upon something. If you get a positive response, however, then this is great news because all you have to do now is to satisfy the condition and the sale is closed. In this way trial closing questions avoid showdowns while still moving you closer to a sale. In short, they're dynamite! Use them liberally throughout your sales presentation as a means of 'testing out the temperature of the sale' whenever you receive a weak buying signal from the customer. You'll create more closing situations and you'll make more sales.

Skill acquisition exercise

Identify the weak buying signals you typically receive from your customers and work out the best type of trial-closing question you could ask in response to each one. Role-play with a colleague of friend until your trial closing questions become a reflex response.

35 Full close after a strong buying signal

A full-closing question is when you ask for the sale outright, and the time to ask it is when you receive your cue from the customer in the form of a strong buying signal. A strong buying signal is anything a customer says or does which suggests a clear interest in making a purchase. When a customer gives you a strong buying signal it usually means they are more or less ready and waiting for you to ask a full-closing question. So don't disappoint your customer! Look them straight in the eye, lean forwards a little and lower your voice to draw them in, and then with an air of confident expectation, ask for the sale. There are two main types of full close: the direct close and the alternative-choice close.

The direct close

The direct close is when you simply go right ahead and ask the customer if he or she would like to buy. Here are a couple of examples:

> Customer: *It looks perfect!* (strong buying signal)

> Salesperson: *Great! Can I write up your order?* (direct close)

> Customer: *So how much is it?* (strong buying signal)

> Salesperson: *It's £499. Would you like one?* (direct close)

I am absolutely convinced that there's no better close than the direct close. It might not be very sophisticated, but it's straightforward, assertive, positive, plain and simple. Therein lies its power.

The alternative-choice close

Another type of full close is the alternative-choice close. This close is most effective when the amount of positive stimuli coming across from your customer is so overwhelming that you can be sure that their strong buying signal indicates that they have already made up their mind to buy. So, rather than asking directly if they would like to buy, instead you ask about their preference regarding some relatively minor aspect of their purchase, such as their preferred method of payment, their preferred date of delivery or their preferred colour. It really doesn't matter what aspect of your product or service you ask about, just as long as it provides the customer with an opportunity to express their preference between two genuine alternative purchase choices. To go back to our previous buying-signal examples, here's how the alternative-choice close could be used:

Customer: *It looks perfect!* (strong buying signal)

Salesperson: *Great! Would you prefer to take delivery this Thursday or next Thursday?* (alternative-choice close)

Customer: *So how much is it?* (strong buying signal)

Salesperson: *It's £499. Would you prefer the white or the satin finish?* (alternative-choice close)

The beauty of the alternative-choice close is that whichever option the customer chooses represents a watertight commitment to go ahead with their purchase. Sold!

Skill acquisition exercise

Identify the strong buying signals that you typically receive from your customers and work out the best type of full-closing question that you could ask in response to each one. Role-play with a colleague or friend until your full-closing questions become a reflex response.

---

36 'Manufacture' a close

When it comes to the number and quality of buying signals that you will receive throughout your career as a professional salesperson, the good news is that you are in charge! This is because just about every buying signal you get from a customer (whether a strong one or a weak one) will be the result of good selling on your part. To put in another way, when you sell well and trigger a customer's interest in making a purchase, he or she will almost always 'reward' you with a buying signal – thereby providing you with the perfect opportunity to ask a closing question of one type or another.

Now for the not-so-good news. Sometimes, no matter how well you sell, that all-important buying signal just isn't forthcoming! This is because from time to time you will inevitably encounter one of those difficult customers who could be described as the 'strong and silent' personality type. Such customers tend to be unresponsive during the course of a sales presentation, typically displaying nothing more than the merest hint of a buying signal. So in these situations you need to be able to 'manufacture' for yourself a legitimate closing opportunity. This can be done by using an approach known as the 'three-question closing sequence'.

The best time to deploy this approach is normally towards the end of a sales presentation after you have explained all the benefits and when, having received very little by way of meaningful feedback from your customer, there's no apparent reason why they should not go ahead with their purchase. So, after a short pause, the three-question closing sequence goes like this:

Salesperson's first question: *Tell me Andrew, have I given you all the information you need?*

Customer: *Yes, I think so.*

Salesperson's second question: *Good, and are you happy with everything?*

Customer: *Well, er ... yes, I think so. Yes.*

Salesperson's third question: *Excellent! Can we go ahead then?'* (direct close)

or

Salesperson's third question: *Excellent! So, when would you prefer to take delivery ... this Thursday or next Thursday?* (alternative-choice close)

The beauty of the three-question closing sequence is that providing your customer responds positively to each of the first two questions then you have effectively succeeded in 'manufacturing' for yourself a strong buying signal and the opportunity to ask a full-closing question. Better still, a 'yes' response to each of the first two questions means that, to all intents and purposes, your customer is already committed to saying 'yes' to your third question and to going ahead with their purchase. If, however, your customer responds negatively to either of the first two questions then at least you're in a great position to be able to find out exactly what else you have to do to make the sale. Here's your script:

- If you get a negative response to your first question:

  OK, so tell me, what additional information do you need?

- If you get a negative response to your second question:

  OK, so tell me, what exactly is it that you're not happy about?

I firmly believe that all salespeople should learn to master the three-question closing sequence. It's easy to use and when executed in the right way and at the right time it always moves you closer to a sale. Best of all, by enabling you to 'manufacture' a closing situation it can help to unlock a sale with even the most unresponsive and difficult of customers.

Skill acquisition exercise

Study the precise wording of the three-question closing sequence as outlined above and check that you feel entirely comfortable with it. If not, feel free to modify it a little. Then memorize it word for word.

---

37 Deploy the summary-of-benefits close

The longer a sales meeting takes and the more involved it becomes due to the complexity of the customer's requirements, the greater the potential effectiveness of this close.

A summary-of-benefits close is when you reflect back on the course of your discussion and pull things together by reminding the customer of all the benefits of your offer that match their specific buying needs – thereby setting yourself up to ask for the sale using a full-closing question. So this close relies completely on being able to accurately recall, in detail, all the key points of your preceding discussions with a customer! That's why in order to ensure that you don't forget anything, immediately prior to deploying this close, it's extremely useful to be able to refer back to some brief notes you made earlier in your discussion.

The first stage in successfully executing this close is to signal to your customer what you're about to do. Let's take the example of a salesperson selling specialist computer systems. While beginning to flick back through their notes, he or she might say:

OK Heather, we seem to have covered everything. So, let's review all the key points we've discussed ...

Depending on the situation, the next stage is then to use either a single-step or multi-step approach. Let's take a closer look at each one:

The single-step approach

The idea behind this approach is to summarize all the key benefits to the customer in a concisely worded statement. Without stopping to pause, you then simply go ahead and ask a full-closing question. The best time to use a single-step approach is when your customer has already given you their explicit agreement to each of the main matching benefits on offer during the course of your previous discussion, leaving you with the simple task of re-stating them. So, in our example, the specialist computer system salesperson might say:

> *You estimated the YP3000 system will save about eight hours per week of staff time, representing an instant reduction in your annual wages bill of £3,000. You also calculated that the eradication of human error saves you about £25 per week, which translates into a further £1,300 of annual savings. Most of all you say you want the total peace of mind that comes with our unique five-star service programme. So ... would you like to go ahead?*

The multi-step approach

Just as with the single-step approach, the idea behind the multi-step approach is to summarize all the key benefits to the customer that have been discussed. The difference is that with this approach you're going to wrap up the customer's agreement to each benefit one by one as you run through your summary. This approach is sometimes referred to as the 'continuous-yes' close because by re-stating each benefit in the form of a loaded 'say yes' question and stacking them all up one after the other your customer will be encouraged to say 'yes' when you conclude your summary with a full-closing question.

The best time to use a multi-step approach is when, up to this point, your customer has only given you their tacit agreement to each of the main matching benefits, leaving you with the need for him or her to affirm them before you feel you can legitimately go for a full close. So, to go back to our example, the specialist computer salesperson might say:

Salesperson: *You estimated the YP3000 system will save about eight hours per week of staff time, representing an instant reduction in your annual wages bill of around £3,000, didn't you?*

Customer: *Yes, I did.*

Salesperson: *OK, and you also calculated that the eradication of human error saves you about £25 per week, which translates into a further £1,300 of annual savings ... is that right?*

Customer: *Yes, that's right*

Salesperson: *Right, and most of all, you say you want the total peace of mind that comes with our unique five-star service programme ... don't you?*

Customer: *Yes, I do.*

Salesperson: *Excellent! So ... would you like to go ahead?*

Skill acquisition exercise

Paying close attention to your use of appropriate body language (gestures, posture, facial expressions, etc.) and to your use of an appropriate tone of voice, role-play both versions of the summary-of-benefits close with a colleague or friend.

---

38 Perfect the art of silence

The golden rule of closing is this:

Once you have asked a full-closing question, keep quiet and make sure it is the customer who speaks next.

The subtle pressure of silence is the only type of pressure that's perfectly acceptable in customer-oriented selling. After all, you've probably worked hard to 'earn' the opportunity to ask a full-closing question, so why shouldn't you be entitled to a reply?

Believe me, you don't want to break this golden rule. Let's look at what happens if you do by taking the example of a fleet-car salesperson. After a long meeting he or she is attempting to close an order for 20 new cars with a large corporate customer:

> Customer: *Hmmm ... I must say your overall offer looks very tempting ...* (strong buying signal)

> Salesperson: *Yes, and with good reason, Michael. It meets all your company's requirements and much more. So ... would you like to go ahead?* (full close)

> Customer: (Takes a deep breath but says nothing – at this point there's a long and drawn-out silence.)

> Salesperson: *Or ... perhaps you're still uncertain about the period of lease?* (breaks the silence)

> Customer: *Yes, maybe you're right. I should think some more about that and anyway, I don't have to make a final decision until the end of the month ...* (The customer's thoughts are now fully re-focused away from having to make a decision.)

Can you see what just happened? When the salesperson in our example broke the silence simply because they had become a little impatient and twitchy, the customer's mind was effectively deflected away from having to make a final decision. To put it bluntly, at the critical moment the salesperson let their customer off the hook. So, once you've asked a closing question, you should always keep quiet and give your customer all the time he or she needs to respond.

Maintaining a silence in those critical moments after a close might sound easy but it is not! If a customer doesn't give you an answer straight away, don't be too surprised if your nerves begin to jangle, your confidence evaporates and you start to experience a powerful urge to say something – anything – in order to relieve the uncomfortable feeling that grows within you as the silence continues. The fact is, the ability to stay cool, calm and confident having asked a closing question is something we have to learn.

At the risk of contradicting myself, it has to be said that occasionally, when a silence has gone on for so long that you can actually see the customer begin to struggle with the strain of having to make their decision, then it may well be appropriate to break the silence yourself. If this is the case, then simply put a big grin on your face and say:

Michael, I've always believed that silence is equal to consent ... am I right?

It's a cheeky way of momentarily relieving the tension for your customer while simultaneously re-focusing them on having to make a decision.

Skill acquisition exercise

Compose a short affirmation that you can repeat quietly to yourself immediately after you ask a closing question. One that will encourage you to stay silent and give your customer plenty of time to make up their mind.

---

39 Help your customer to make up their mind

If a customer is genuinely experiencing some real difficulty in making up their mind, this approach can work wonders. Also known as the 'weigh-up' close, it's when you suggest to the customer that perhaps the best way to resolve their dilemma is to weigh up all the positives against all the negatives of their decision by writing them down. For example:

Susan, I can understand that this is a tough decision for you so I'd like to suggest that we go through the process of weighing up all the positives and negatives of your decision ... just to see if we can clear the fog one way or the other ... shall we give it a try?

Then take a blank sheet of paper and draw a vertical line straight down the middle. In large letters at the top of the right-hand column write 'Yes, I'll buy' and at the top of the left-hand column write 'No, I won't buy'. (Note: it is important to use these exact words because this makes it perfectly clear to your customer that they will be expected to make a final decision one way or the other.) Next, your task is to tactfully and skilfully direct the customer's thinking so that his or her list of reasons for going ahead with a purchase clearly outweigh the list of reasons against.

If your customer is struggling to make up their mind between buying from you or buying from one of your competitors, you could try using an adaptation of this approach. Once again take a large blank sheet of paper and draw a vertical line down the middle. This time, however, the column headings should read 'I'll buy from (write in your own name)' in the right-hand column and 'I'll buy from them' in the left-hand column. Once again, it is important that you use these exact words because in a subtle way it personalizes their decision. As before, it is then up to you as the salesperson to encourage your customer to end up with more reasons why they should buy from you instead of the competition.

Here's a little tip: this close works best if you hand over to your customer the responsibility for filling out the two columns so that they feel in control of the 'weighing-up' process. It's also important to start off by asking your customer to list all the positive reasons first, while still fresh in their mind. Put it like this:

> *Let's start off by writing under the right-hand column all the reasons you can think of for placing your business with me today.*

Clearly, the key to your success with this technique is being well prepared. Not only will you need to know about all the benefits and potential drawbacks of your product or service but you will also need to be exceptionally adept and well rehearsed in the way you assist your customer through the list-making process. The fact is, using this approach is only believable to a customer if they perceive that you are genuinely considering both sides of the equation and have their best interests at heart. It's a real skill to be able to help a customer to come up with a comprehensive list of reasons without seeming to apply any pressure or being too pushy. However, it can be done and when, in the final analysis, a 'yes' decision clearly outweighs a 'no', the sale is effectively closed.

Skill acquisition exercise

Write out (a) all the benefits, and (b) all the potential drawbacks of your product or service. Then rehearse how you will lead your customer through the list-development process, and in such a way that they will feel as though it's their list, not yours.

40 Cultivate the right closing vocabulary

When you're about to gain a customer's agreement, every word you say counts. Let's take a look at why it's better to use some words in preference to others.

Don't say 'contract', say 'agreement form' or 'paperwork'

Think about the word 'contract' from a customer's point of view. Most people are extremely wary of a contract. It just sounds too formal and legalistic. So, instead, call it an 'agreement form' or 'the paperwork' because these terms sound a lot less scary.

Don't say 'sign', say 'authorize' or 'autograph'

People tend to feel a little nervous if they are asked to 'sign' something (especially if it's a 'contract'). It just sounds too serious. That's why it's preferable to ask a customer to 'authorize' or ' autograph' the agreement form. These terms are more customer-friendly. What's more, by using these terms it's as if, as a matter of courtesy, you are simply acknowledging their buying authority or status.

Don't say 'pay', say 'invest'

The word 'pay' has negative connotations for most customers because it puts the emphasis on the amount that your product or service will cost them. The word 'invest', on the other hand, has more positive connotations because it puts the emphasis on the value that your price represents and on the benefits that your product or service will provide. Somehow it seems much more sensible to invest in something than to pay for it.

Don't say 'price', say 'total investment'

The word 'price' can easily strike the wrong chord with some customers because it has connotations of sacrifice or loss. The term 'total investment' on the other hand, is much more positive because it infers desirability and worth.

Don't say 'buy', say 'own'

It is usually wise to avoid the word 'buy'. It's a word that can easily touch the wrong nerve for customers simply because it reminds them of the need to exchange their hard-earned money in order to obtain your product or service. So it's preferable to ask your customers if they would like to 'own' it. Deep down in a customer's psyche, the thought of 'owning' something triggers a much warmer feeling than the thought of buying something.

Skill acquisition exercise

Identify the key words and phrases that you habitually use when seeking a customer's agreement and finalizing a sale. Make an assessment of them and decide which ones could be usefully substituted with a more customer-friendly choice.

---

41 Ensure the sale is properly CLOSED

A well-closed sale is one that leaves your customer feeling great about having chosen to do business with you. The acronym CLOSED is a good way to remember the ideal sequence of events for ensuring this happens every time. It goes like this…

C = Congratulate your customer

As soon as your customer has said 'yes' to going ahead with a purchase (and I mean the precise moment the word has left their lips) you should put a big smile on your face and offer your heartfelt congratulations. For example:

That's fantastic, John. Congratulations.

L = Legitimize their decision

Make a point of reinforcing the wisdom of their decision. This is especially important if they have had a tough time making up their mind to buy from you. For example:

I'm absolutely certain you've made the right decision.

O = Offer a congratulatory handshake

The simple act of offering to shake the customer's hand demonstrates how pleased you are that they have made the right decision and communicates that you are genuinely appreciative of their business. At the same time the symbolic value of 'shaking hands on a deal' has the effect of locking in your customer's commitment to their decision.

S = Say thank you

Said with genuine sincerity, these words are among the most powerful in any salesperson's toolkit, and the time to say them is right now. For example:

... and thanks very much for placing your order with us. I really appreciate it.

E = Explain what happens next

Depending on the type of product or service you sell there may well be a number of follow-through steps post-sale. If so, at this point it will be necessary to briefly run through them one more time in order to confirm all the details. For example:

Within 48 hours you'll receive a written confirmation of your order. As we've agreed, your machine will be scheduled for delivery on the 15th of November and our installation team will arrive the next day. They'll set it up, and take you through all the operating instructions.

D = Deal with the payment

Now you can go ahead and take your customer's payment. For example:

Now, I just need you to authorize the paperwork and then we can get the ball rolling.

42 Time your exit

There are three rules for timing your exit to perfection. Let's take a look at each one:

Rule one

The moment a sale is successfully completed it is only natural for both you and your new customer to experience a mild sense of euphoria. Any tension quickly dissipates, which means there's often a strong temptation to accept an offer of another cup of coffee and to stay for a little while longer. However, at this point it is important to observe the first rule of timing your exit:

> **When I close a sale, the best time to say goodbye**
> **is while we're both still on a high.**

Once you have congratulated your customer on his or her decision, made arrangements for delivery as necessary and finalized the payment, there's nothing left to do except to say goodbye and make a swift exit. By staying even a moment longer than necessary, there's always a danger that you could mess things up and undo all your good work. You never know. The customer might have a sudden afterthought or ask an awkward question. Worse still, you might unconsciously say or do something which causes them to reconsider their decision. You cannot improve on 100 per cent success. That's why there are no exceptions to this rule – no matter how friendly your customer appears to be and no matter how sure you are that the sale is watertight!

Rule two

The second rule of timing your exit relates to a different set of circumstances. It's very tempting only ever to think of 'closing' in terms of closing the sale. However, while this is certainly your primary objective, restricting your thinking in this way can dramatically reduce your overall sales performance. The fact is that sometimes (for a variety of customer-related reasons) it is just not possible to close a sale. So under these circumstances you must trust your instincts and choose the right moment to switch direction and attempt to close on your next best secondary or 'fall-back' objective. A good secondary objective at least takes you one step closer to a sale at a later date. Some classic examples include:

- Arrange for a full product demonstration.
- Agree to submit a formal written proposal.
- Organize a factory visit.
- Arrange to do a comprehensive cost–benefit survey.
- Promise to find out more information.
- Agree to renew contact at a future point in time.

Since some secondary objectives are preferable to others, you'll need to be crystal clear about your priorities. That way, if for some good reason you can't achieve your best secondary objective then you can shoot for your next best and so on. This ensures that you will always walk away from a sale secure in the knowledge that you have achieved the best possible outcome. So here's the second rule of timing your exit:

> When I can't close a sale, the best time to say goodbye
> is as soon as I've achieved my best secondary objective.

Rule three

Occasionally, in the middle of a sales presentation you will realize that your product or service is not at all well matched to that particular customer's requirements. In these situations there's simply no point in continuing with the sale, even if, as is sometimes the case, your customer is blissfully unaware of the extent of the problem! The only ethical course of action is to explain the situation to your customer straight away, recommend a different solution if you can, and then pack up your things and say goodbye. So the third rule of timing your exit goes like this:

> When I realize it's not a good buy for my customer,
> it's time to say 'goodbye' to my customer.

Skill acquisition exercise

Identify three potentially useful secondary objectives. List them in priority order. Memorize your list and resolve that you'll act upon it whenever you find yourself unable to achieve your primary objective of making a sale.

Summary

In this chapter we have looked at how to:

- tune in to buying signals
- trial close after a weak buying signal
- full close after a strong buying signal
- 'manufacture' a close
- deploy the summary-of-benefits close
- perfect the art of silence
- help your customer to make up their mind
- cultivate the right closing vocabulary
- ensure the sale is properly CLOSED
- time your exit.

05

objection-handling-phase selling skills

In this chapter you will learn:
- how to handle the customer's objection to their complete satisfaction and, if possible, turn it around into a closing opportunity.

Opening phase
Set the scene for a businesslike and mutually beneficial conversation to take place between you and the customer.

Interviewing phase
Find out all about the customer's specific needs and wants, and uncover the key benefits that they are really looking for.

Matching phase
Match the customer's needs and wants as closely as possible to the benefits of your product or service offer.

Closing phase
Get the customer's agreement to go ahead, and leave them feeling positive about their purchase decision.

Objection-handling phase
Handle the customer's objection to their complete satisfaction and, if possible, turn it around into a closing opportunity.

43 Condition yourself positively to objections

An objection is when a customer responds negatively to your proposition. Objections typically relate to an aspect of your product, your service or your price that a customer perceives to be mismatched to their requirements in some way – either in absolute terms or by comparison to a competitor's offer. Here are some classic examples:

- *The control panel on your machine is too complicated ...* (product-based objection stated in absolute terms)
- *The control panel on your machine is more complicated than the XYZ Company's machine ...* (same objection stated in comparative terms)
- *I don't think your firm has sufficient technical expertise in this area ...* (service-based objection stated in absolute terms)
- *I don't think your firm has as much technical expertise in this area as the XYZ Company ...* (same objection stated in comparative terms)
- *Your price is very expensive ...* (price-based objection stated in absolute terms)
- *Your price is a lot more expensive than the XYZ Company ...* (same objection stated in comparative terms)

Many salespeople live in fear of objections because they believe customers use them to deliberately block a sale. The trouble is, when salespeople condition themselves negatively to objections in this way, their insecurity inevitably reveals itself during their sales presentations. They often become visibly pale at the mere thought of an objection, let alone at the mention of one, and so do everything possible to avoid having to confront them. This usually means they talk far too much, hardly letting their customers get a word in edgeways. They'll even ignore an objection altogether if they think they can possibly get away with it. Then when they finally reach the point where they have no option but to answer an objection, they do so almost apologetically. Under these circumstances a customer's faith in both the salesperson and in their offer quickly dissipates. The point is, for these salespeople, losing the sale actually becomes a self-fulfilling prophecy.

By contrast, top salespeople adopt a completely different mindset. Unlike their lesser-performing counterparts they condition themselves positively to objections, to the point where they actually welcome them as opportunities to dispel any doubts in their customer's mind, and to clear a path towards the sale. This attitude similarly translates across into their sales presentations. They readily and confidently discuss their customer's objections and as a result, they earn their customer's trust and close more sales.

The key to conditioning yourself positively to objections is to look at them from a customer's perspective. Ask yourself 'If I were a customer, why would I want to raise an objection?'. As soon as you do this you'll realize that it's perfectly natural for a genuine buyer to want to raise an objection and for any number of good reasons. For example, most people become hesitant and critically evaluative of an important purchase decision because they have to be able to fully justify the expenditure to themselves and sometimes to others too. Quite understandably, they also feel the need to have a thorough comprehension of all aspects of an offer before they will feel comfortable about making a decision to buy. In fact, when you really think about it, the more genuine a customer is, the more likely it is that he or she would want to raise an objection. Wouldn't you agree?

So, from now on, choose to see every objection for what it really is: a buying signal! Although it's extremely well 'disguised' or 'encoded' as an objection, nine times out of ten, this is what it really is:

- a request for more detailed information
- a need for further clarification and explanation
- a sign that a specific area is of special importance or interest
- a misconception or misunderstanding that needs clearing up
- a request for help and advice in making a more informed decision
- a need for additional reassurance about something.

Armed with this mindset you can look forward to welcoming your customer's objections because each and every one is a golden opportunity to put your customer's mind at rest and to clear a path towards closing the sale.

Skill acquisition exercise

Repeat the following affirmation quietly to yourself, over and over, until it becomes a deeply held belief:

Beneath every objection under the sun, lies an opportunity for a sale to be won.

---

44 Pre-handle predictable objections

Pre-handling an objection means that you yourself raise the objection. The advantage of doing this is twofold. Firstly, you get to control the timing of the objection. The whole point of pre-handling an objection is to get a particular issue out of the way early on in your sales presentation when it is less likely to interfere with the customer's final purchase decision. Secondly, a customer does not feel as though he or she 'owns' an objection that was raised by the salesperson, which means that your customer is less likely to feel the need to 'dig their heels in' and defend it – because you raised it. Here's an example:

Example

Mary sells accountancy services for a large firm. One of her target customer groups are small-business entrepreneurs. With these customers she knows there's one objection that's guaranteed to crop up every time. For a variety of reasons they are always extremely nervous about the idea of doing business with a large firm. However, with experience, Mary has learned that the best way to deal with this objection is to pre-handle it, and at a very early stage in her presentation. The dialogue goes something like this:

Mary: ... *Incidentally, I know that some of my small-business clients, entrepreneurs like yourself, have initially felt a little uncomfortable with the idea of handing over their company records to a large accountancy firm like ours. So may I ask you, is that something that concerns you at all, Michael?*

Customer: *Frankly, yes, maybe it does a little ... let's just say we're naturally cautious about giving away any commercially sensitive information.*

Mary: *Fair enough, I can certainly understand your reservations. However, what our small-business clients soon discover is that it's precisely because of our size that we've been able to develop state-of-the-art data protection systems for ensuring that our client information is always kept completely and totally secure. Tell me, does that help to put your mind at ease, Michael?*

Customer: *Well yes, when you put it like that, I suppose it does.*

Mary: *Good, and is there anything else that concerns you about that ... because if so, perhaps we should discuss it now before we go any further?*

Customer: *No, I guess not.*

Mary: *That's great. I'm glad I've had a chance to put your mind at rest on that one. Now, where were we ... ?* (Mary now resumes her presentation.)

Let's review the finer points of executing this technique:

1 Make it perfectly clear that you're only bringing it up because in the past you've found it to be a common concern among customers.
2 Enquire if the issue is similarly a matter of concern for your customer, and in such a way that makes it easy for him or her to say 'yes' without feeling foolish or embarrassed.
3 If the customer admits that it is a concern for them, cover it by referring to past customers' experiences.
4 Check that the customer agrees with what you've said and that there aren't any other surrounding concerns.
5 Make a point of putting the subject firmly behind you before continuing with your presentation.

Finally, as in the above example, this technique should only ever be applied to 'predictable' objections – those which you know for a fact will come up because they always do. The last thing you want is to bring up an objection that your customer wouldn't have otherwise considered because this would only result in making your job even more challenging than it is already!

45 Play CATCH with every objection raised

Successful objection-handling is not like being in a boxing match! Your aim is not to hit the customer back as hard as you can in the hope that you can quickly eliminate their concern with one knockout counter-punch! On the contrary, it's about going through a step-by-step objection-handling process to slowly but surely dismantle any doubt in your customer's mind, and, whenever possible, turn it around into a closing opportunity. That's why it's a lot more like playing a game of catch-the-ball with your customers than it is about trading punches with them. Your aim is to CATCH every objection raised and then throw it back and forth a few times in order to be able to handle it in a respectful, customer-friendly and professional manner. Using the acronym CATCH, here's how:

C = Clarify it

First make sure that you fully understand the objection. This can be done by encouraging the customer to tell you as much as possible about it. Most people find it difficult to communicate the precise nature of their concerns within their first few sentences, so it is important to realize that you'll often need to question the objection in order to make it specific. That way, you'll have something much more concrete to work with. For example:

> Customer: *I don't like the sound of that kind of deal ... I never have.* (This objection is couched in general terms only.)

> Salesperson: *Tell me more Bob, what exactly is it you don't like the sound of?*

An alternative technique is simply to repeat back to the customer your understanding of the specific point(s) being made in order to check that you have interpreted it correctly. For example, you may say:

> *Let me just check I've understood you correctly, Bob, are you saying that … ?*

Sometimes it becomes apparent that there is actually more than one objection being raised. In these cases you have no choice but to go ahead and help the customer to articulate the exact nature of their concerns. Even if this results in the identification of two or three separate objections, so be it. At least you will have found out the precise nature of the objections you are going to have to deal with in order to make a sale.

A = Agree with the logic behind it

The second step is always to tell the customer that you think their point is a valid one, and why. This does not mean you should agree with the objection itself, only with the logic behind it. By doing this you are investing in the customer's self-esteem and thereby helping to soften your counter-response and make it easier for him or her to accept. Some useful phrases are:

- *Yes, I do understand your concern because …*
- *Yes, I can appreciate your logic because …*
- *Yes, in theory you're quite right because …*
- *Yes, in a way that is perfectly true because …*

T = Trial close on it

As we have already noted, a top salesperson regards every genuine objection as if it were a subtle buying signal (although often very well disguised!) around which to wrap a trial-closing question. So, whenever appropriate, the third step is to trial close on the objection before going on to counter it. For example, you might say:

> *Bob, just supposing I could answer that point to your complete and total satisfaction, then would you be happy to go ahead?*

If the customer agrees, then the sale is effectively closed subject to the objection being handled to their satisfaction. On the other hand, if the customer responds negatively you must probe further to find out what else is holding them back, and then trial close again on both points.

C = Counter it

The fourth step in handling an objection is to counter it. This can be done in one of three ways:

1 You can *drown it*, by explaining how in their situation the advantages would by far outweigh the disadvantages.
2 You can *dilute it*, by explaining how, in practice, it would not prove to be such a serious problem for them.
3 You can *dissolve it*, by explaining how it would not apply in their particular case.

There is no reason why you should not be able to anticipate virtually all the objections you are likely to encounter, and rehearse your counter responses to perfection. It's up to you to make sure you are well prepared.

H = Harvest it

The final step is to ask the customer whether you have answered their objection to their complete and total satisfaction. If the answer is 'no' then you have no option but to find out why and try once again to answer it in a way that satisfies them. If, on the other hand, the answer is 'yes' then you have two options:

1 If, when the objection was first raised, you chose not to trial close on it for some reason, then you should 'bury' the objection once and for all so that he or she may never raise it again, before returning to your presentation. For example, you might say:

   I'm glad we've cleared that up, Bob ... Now, where were we?

2 If, when the objection was first raised, you had decided to wrap a trial-closing question around it (i.e. subject to their complete satisfaction with your answer, they had agreed to go ahead), then you've made a sale. All you have to do now is take the order!

46 Flush out the real objection

Some customers have a tendency to reel off any number of 'smokescreen' objections. They're so called because in reality they're not that important to the customer. The truth is they're usually just convenient excuses that serve only to camouflage a customer's genuine indecision about a much deeper, underlying concern; an issue that he or she doesn't want to tell you about for fear of having to confront it and actually make a decision. Since it's very easy to end up wasting a lot of time trying to answer what are effectively 'fob off' objections, you have to learn to trust your instincts. If you can sense a customer isn't being entirely candid about their concerns then the only way forward is to try and cut through the smokescreen and find out what's really holding them back. One way to do this is to put a smokescreen objection 'on ice' in order to try and winkle out the real objection. For example, you might say:

> *Janet, I do understand the point you're making, but leaving it to one side just for the moment ... I just get the feeling there's something else that's stopping you from going ahead ... may I ask what it is?*

No matter how hard you try to get a customer to reveal their true objection, occasionally he or she will simply go quiet – and you're left with the feeling that they must be holding back some deep-seated irrational fear that they either can't or won't tell you about. Maybe it's the fear of making a commitment, of what someone else might think, or of trying out something new. Regardless, you have little option but to probe for the fear and help your customer to voice it and confront it. Understandably, it's not easy for people to reveal the underlying fears and anxieties that affect their decisions, so you'll need to probe for them with great tact and sensitivity. Here's how to go about it.

First, you need to ask for the customer's permission to be perfectly candid and open about something that is on your mind. This shows respect for your customer and signals to him or her that you would like to take the conversation onto a deeper and more intimate level. Second, you need to go ahead and probe for the fear. In order to do this, I believe a straight closed question works best because by being direct, honest and specific about your suspicions, a customer is much more likely to respond than if you ask a more searching open-ended style of question. In phrasing the question, it's also important that you use the kind of language that seeks to 'connect' with your customer on an emotional level. For example, you could say:

> *I'm sensing that there's something really bothering you Janet ... tell me, is it the fear of trying out something new?*

or

> *I'm concerned that you seem to be worried about something Janet ... tell me, is it the fear of learning to use a new technology?*

Sometimes the only way to unlock a difficult sale is to 'go fishing' in the hope that you can flush out the customer's underlying concerns. The great thing about using these techniques is that when your customer finally reveals their real objection, it usually comes complete with flashing lights and a siren. In other words, by reading the customer's body language and other cues the chances are that it will be very obvious that you've succeeded in flushing it out. At this point, at last, both you and your customer will have taken a giant leap towards being able to conclude the sale one way or the other.

Skill acquisition exercise

Create a list of all the 'fob off' objections you're likely to encounter. In each case, decide how you can cut through the smokescreen and flush out your customer's real, underlying concerns.

47 Use arithmetic to handle price objections

There are two keys to successfully handling price objections. The first key is to accept responsibility for the fact that your customer has seen fit to raise a price objection. This means adopting the attitude that you obviously haven't yet convinced the customer of the true value-for-money that your price represents for them. The second key is to go ahead and do the convincing. This can be done most effectively by using one or more of the four calculation tools of adding, dividing, subtracting and multiplying.

Adding and dividing are the perfect tools to use whenever a customer raises a price objection stated in absolute terms, such as 'Your price is very expensive.' Here's how:

Add

Add up every feature and benefit to justify and defend the financial value of your price right down to the last penny. For example:

> So you can be sure of exactly what you'd be getting for your money, let's run through each of the key features and benefits, and the financial value they'll bring to your business ...

Divide

Divide your price by the life expectancy of your product – then 'reduce to the ridiculous', such as the price per day. Once you've done this then you can go on to make it sound trivial by comparing it with an everyday purchase such as a cup of coffee or a newspaper. For example:

> You said you'd expect our machine to last for about five years, so your total investment of £1,250 works out to be £250 year. When divided by 50 working weeks per year that works out to be £5 a week ... and that's the equivalent of only a pound a day ... about half the price of a cup of coffee!

Now let's consider subtracting and multiplying. They're the perfect tools to adopt whenever a customer raises a price objection stated in comparative terms, such as 'Your price is a lot more expensive than the XYZ Company.' Here's how to use them:

Subtract

Subtract the features and benefits the customer wants but will not get by buying cheaper from your competitor. For example:

Let's take a closer look at all the features and benefits you've said you wanted, but won't get by buying cheaper ... firstly, you won't get the total peace of mind that comes with our unique five-star customer-service programme; secondly, you won't get ... (and so on).

Multiply

Multiply the hidden costs of buying a cheaper product or service in the mind of the customer. In other words, heighten the customer's apprehensions and uncertainties about the implications of buying cheaper. For example:

Tell me Michael, next time there's a breakdown emergency in your factory and you urgently need a service engineer, then what price is the peace of mind that comes with a reputation for dependability like ours?

By using these tools of basic arithmetic you have the means to overcome virtually any price objection. However, the real power of these tools lies in your ability to use them creatively and imaginatively – and if necessary, in combination with each other – to put your customer's mind totally at rest about the true value-for-money that your price represents.

Skill acquisition exercise

Anticipate all the price objections you're likely to encounter and then use the four tools of adding, dividing, subtracting and multiplying to prepare your best responses in advance. Rehearse carrying them out, and commit them to memory.

---

48 Seek out your customer's advice

Do you remember Murphy's Law? It states that, in life, just when you least expect it, if something can go wrong, it will – and usually at the most inopportune moment. Here's how it comes up in sales:

Example

I'd been in with an important customer for quite some time. Everything seemed to have gone well and I'd been able to resolve two or three major customer concerns during the course of my presentation and to her total satisfaction. Then, without warning – Murphy's Law – I could hardly believe my ears as she suddenly came up with an unusual yet authentic-sounding objection that I'd never encountered before and to which I hadn't a clue how to respond.

It's just a fact of business life that from time to time an unusual objection will crop up that takes you completely by surprise – and yes, infuriatingly, it only ever seems to happen in those situations when everything else meets with the customer's approval and it's apparently the only remaining obstacle preventing them from going ahead! So, here's what to do about it: look your customer directly in the eye, and in a disarmingly forthright way, simply tell the truth and ask for their help. For example:

*Heather, that's a very good point you raise and quite honestly I just don't know what to suggest ... so let me ask you, have you yourself got any ideas as to what could be done about it ... what would **you** suggest?*

The beauty of this approach is that you will soon find out how important the objection really is. You see, if it is genuinely important, your customer will probably go deep into thought and do their level best to come up with a solution. This in itself is an excellent sign because irrespective of whether or not he or she comes up with a solution on the spot, at least you now know exactly what you have to do to successfully close the sale. If it is relatively unimportant, however, then after a brief moment of reflection the customer will probably just dismiss it as something minor, removing the need for you to have to deal with it and so clearing your path towards closing the sale.

Incidentally, if it transpires that the objection is important and there's no obvious way to resolve it, tell the customer that you'll return to your office to consult with your colleagues, and that you'll do your very best to come up with a solution. Most importantly, arrange a date and time for a return visit when you can report back to your customer, and always take the opportunity to trial close on the objection before leaving. Here's your script:

Heather, providing I can resolve this issue to your complete satisfaction when I come back to see you, then can I take it that everything else is OK and you'll be happy to place your business with me at that time?

Skill acquisition exercise

In the event that a customer should raise an unusual objection that would be impossible to anticipate, decide upon the exact wording of a question you could comfortably ask that would seek their advice for dealing with it. Practise and memorize it.

---

49 Trade a minor price concession

Do you ever encounter a type of customer known as a 'priceshaver'? Despite the fact that you've matched all their requirements and addressed all their concerns, this is the type of customer who persists in pushing you to shave a few pounds off the price, almost as if their life depends on it!

In handling the priceshaver, your initial response should always be to defend the value-to-the-customer that your price-package represents and to maintain the integrity of your company's pricing policy. Unfortunately, however, it's the very nature of a priceshaver to 'dig their heels in' and to just keep on pushing for a price concession, regardless. It's a pig-headed attitude that defies all logic. There's something else about a priceshaver customer that you should know: the moment an unsuspecting and inexperienced salesperson buckles under the pressure and agrees to an unqualified price concession, no matter how small it might be, the priceshaver will simply take it, say 'thanks very much', and then keep on pushing for even more until the salesperson has been well and truly taken to the cleaners.

Let's assume then, that you've justified your price to the hilt and that, true to form, your priceshaver customer still refuses to buy without a discount. What now? Well, under these circumstances you could suggest a 'trade' whereby you agree to make a small price concession but only on the condition that you modify your offer accordingly. This approach is based upon the time-honoured principle of sales negotiation: *A slightly different price buys a slightly different package.*

Of course, whatever it is that you propose to deduct from your offer must be of about equal value, in financial terms, to the price concession you're making. Most importantly, it must also be something that your customer won't mind letting go of as a part of your package. In fact, the real key to success when trading a minor price concession is to offer to trade it off against some equally minor element of your package which, to that particular customer at that particular time, is of only minimal value. For example, imagine you were a specialist computer system salesperson. If, during your discussions you'd learnt that your customer is already an experienced computer user, then this would mean they would not necessarily require the full training that is included in your standard price-package. So in this case you could agree to a minor price concession but only on the understanding that he or she spent less time with your computer system trainer.

At this point you might be thinking 'Yes, but what if there is no scope whatsoever for modifying my package – then what?' Well, there is one other trading opportunity that you might want to consider as a last ditch effort: you could try trading a minor price concession for a final agreement. In other words, you could agree to grant your priceshaver customer a minor discount but only on the condition that they give you a 'yes' decision right there and then; no more ifs or buts. As a never-to-be-repeated, take-it-or-leave-it final offer, this can be a useful way, perhaps the only way, to hook a priceshaver. It's your call.

Skill acquisition exercise

Identify the non-price variables that you could suggest to a 'priceshaver' customer as a trade-off against a slightly lower price. Prepare your script for suggesting the trade.

50 Use the ATTACK formula

After a long and hard sales presentation, some customers will just thank you for your time and insist they'll be in touch after they have 'had a chance to think about it'. This is one of the most frustrating and difficult objections to overcome because the customer is not really objecting to the substance of your offer at all. Consequently, you have two basic choices. Depending on your reading of the situation, you can either adopt a defensive stance, which means taking the customer at their word, or you can decide to go on the offensive by using the ATTACK formula. Each letter of this acronym stands for an action in a series of steps that can help you to successfully turn this situation around to your advantage. It goes like this:

A = Ask what areas of doubt still remain

For example:

> *I agree that you should think about it, Michael, although in my experience when people say this it usually means they are still unsure of a few things. May I ask what's on your mind ... ?*

T = Transcribe

Transcribe each of the customer's areas of doubt onto a master list, making sure that you write down every single one, no matter how many there are. For example:

> *OK, let's list them all out and see what we're talking about. Your first concern is X, have I got that right?* (and so on)

T = Trial close before attempting to answer the points on the list

For example:

> *So in a perfect world, if I could deal with all these points to your complete and total satisfaction, then can I take it that you'd be happy to place an order?*

A = Answer

Answer each point, and be sure to check that you have handled it to the customer's complete and total satisfaction. Then ask if you can cross it off the list. For example:

That's great! I'm glad we've cleared that one up Michael, so can I cross it off the list now?

C = Close

When you've crossed the last item off the list, close the sale by using the alternative-choice close. For example:

Fantastic! That's everything covered! So, when would you like to take delivery Michael: this Thursday or the following Thursday?

K = Keep quiet

Keep quiet and don't deflect the customer's mind from making their final decision.

Please note: using the ATTACK formula *cannot* compensate for a poor sales presentation. It is simply a means of encouraging your customer not to procrastinate and, hopefully, to make a positive decision.

Skill acquisition exercise

Role-play with a colleague or friend until you feel confident in being able to use the ATTACK formula the next time a customer insists 'I want to think about it'.

---

51 Resort to a tactic of last resort

At the end of a sales presentation there are two nightmare scenarios that can all too easily unfold. Let's call them scenario Y and scenario Z. The word 'nightmare' sums them up perfectly because these are situations when your customer suddenly and unexpectedly says something that appears to slam the door firmly shut on any remaining hope you had of being able to close the sale. It seems all is lost. Well, perhaps not. In each of these scenarios there is a tactic of last resort that's worth a try.

Scenario Y

If a corporate customer has been unusually quiet throughout your meeting and then coldly informs you they have decided to buy from a major competitor instead of from you ... but is extremely evasive about telling you why, then it's likely there's some form of skulduggery going on. Perhaps he or she is receiving an under-the-table payment in return for placing the order with your competitor, or something of that sort. Unfortunately, regardless of what it is that they are not telling you, by being starved of information you are in a virtually impossible situation and the sale is effectively lost. There is, however, one last-ditch question you could ask:

> *Tell me Sam, in an ideal world, if there was **one** thing I could do to get you to buy from me instead, what would it be?*

The power of this question lies in its phrasing. Providing it is asked in all sincerity, it's a question that always comes across as non-accusing and non-confrontational because your customer can answer safe in the knowledge that whatever he or she says is conditional upon there being an 'ideal world'. Moreover, the fact that you only ask for 'one thing' tends to focus their mind and make it a lot easier to answer than a more general style of question. As soon as you have asked this question you must remain silent and wait patiently for the customer to respond. Chances are you'll probably still receive the same 'stonewall' treatment, but on those occasions when you do get a reply at least you will be in a position to consider your options. With a bit of luck you just might be able to find a way forward to make the sale.

Scenario Z

At the conclusion of a long and laborious sales presentation some customers just say 'no' and insist that you leave without giving you any reason at all for their decision. Typically, however, this has nothing to do with your abilities as a salesperson. More than likely it happens because the customer has a phobia about salespeople. Some people are extremely wary of salespeople. They never let their guard down or allow themselves to enter into a meaningful conversation about their requirements for fear of losing control of their own purchase decision. This creates an extremely frustrating situation! Without the necessary feedback there comes a point when you are powerless to do anything but say goodbye and head for the door. However, since at this point you have absolutely nothing left to lose, there is another tactic of last resort that's worth a try. Here's what to do. Just as you approach the door to leave, turn your head to look back at the customer one last time, and in a tone of voice that suggests it is an afterthought, ask this question:

> *Sam, I wonder if you would be kind enough to do me a big favour ... just so I know exactly where I've gone wrong ... what was the **main reason** you decided not to buy from me today?*

You never know, when the customer's guard is down because they think you've accepted their decision, you might just get a reply that gives you an opportunity to recover the situation.

Skill acquisition exercise

Check that you feel entirely comfortable with the wording of the two questions of last resort outlined above. If not, modify them to suit. Then memorize them word for word, and practise your delivery of each question.

---

52 Bring your customer back down the mountain

Sometimes, working to keep a sale closed is every bit as important as securing it in the first place! If you've ever had the frustrating experience of having a sale cancelled completely 'out of the blue' within a few days because the customer has had second thoughts, then you'll already be familiar with a phenomenon known as PPCD – which stands for Post-Purchase Cognitive Dissonance. The words 'post-purchase' meaning after the moment when the purchase decision was made, 'cognitive' meaning perceiving or being aware of, and 'dissonance' meaning discord or uncertainty.

Generally speaking, a customer will experience PPCD in direct proportion to the degree of importance that he or she has attached to their purchase. That's why (i) the more expensive it is in financial terms, (ii) the more competitive your marketplace is, and (iii) the more complex your products and services are, the more likely it is that a customer will start to question the wisdom of their decision – almost from the moment they authorize the order form! So it's important to have a plan of action at the ready that's capable of 'neutralizing' the threat of PPCD and bringing a customer safely 'back down the mountain' from the heady heights of making a big purchase decision.

In devising a plan to bring your customers 'back down the mountain', you could consider employing one or more of the following actions:

Reaffirm their decision

At the time of making a sale, as soon as you have congratulated the customer on their purchase, make a point of reinforcing the wisdom of their decision by reaffirming all the positive reasons why it's the right choice. Then go on to encourage them to remember those reasons should they have any doubts after you've gone.

Be accessible

Just before saying goodbye, get the customer's assurance that he or she will contact you if they have any further questions, afterthoughts or concerns. Make a point of ensuring that they have all your contact details and especially your 'after hours' telephone number. Tell them that you see it as your job to ensure that your customers always feel 100 per cent happy with their decision.

Make a follow-up telephone call

The day after the sale, telephone your customer to thank them for their order, to check the details of it, and to double-check that they are still totally committed to going ahead with their purchase.

Send a letter

Post or email a thank-you letter to be received by your customer within 24 hours of their purchase decision. In your letter say how much you appreciate their order, confirm the details and go on to take the opportunity to reassure the customer that they have made the right decision. If necessary, mention the many hundreds of satisfied customers who are already using your product or service.

Use a go-between

Within a day or two of the sale, arrange for one of your existing customers who knows your new customer to telephone and congratulate him or her on their new purchase and, most importantly, to endorse the wisdom of their decision.

Skill acquisition exercise

Develop a detailed action plan for keeping a sale closed whenever you anticipate that a new customer is going to experience PPCD.

Summary

In this chapter we have looked at how to:

- condition yourself positively to objections
- pre-handle predictable objections
- play CATCH with every objection raised
- flush out the real objection
- use arithmetic to handle price objections
- seek out your customer's advice
- trade a minor price concession
- use the ATTACK formula
- resort to a tactic of last resort
- bring your customer back down the mountain.

I trust this book has been a stimulating read and that you're already successfully closing more sales. But please don't put it down just yet. Now is the time for further action! If you've not already done so, flick back through the book and make a short list of all those selling skills that you know in your heart you could still improve upon – just for the sake of a little extra effort. Then turn this list into an 'action plan' by putting each skill into priority order and setting yourself a date for re-doing the corresponding *skill acquisition exercise* and trying out your new ideas in the field. This will ensure that you get the very most out of this book.

Looking ahead, in your quest to become a more successful salesperson, your mission is to be constantly striving to improve your selling skills. This can only be done through the discipline of ongoing learning and self-development. As the saying goes:

If I want to earn more, I've got to learn more.

However, as well as the core face-to-face selling skills you've been developing by working through this book, I'd like to encourage you to widen the focus of your learning in the future so that it embraces the full spectrum of selling skills. Specifically, I'm talking about learning how to:

- develop the mindset of an elite salesperson
- become an expert sales prospector
- book more sales appointments by phone
- master the art of sales negotiating
- build strong and rewarding customer relationships.

In the ultra-competitive world of professional selling, if you don't keep on learning you'll soon get left behind by your competitors. So, resolve to become a life-long student of your craft. Keep on reading books, attending training programmes, listening to CDs and watching DVDs. Above all:

Let every customer be your teacher!

Well, you have reached the end of the book but I hope that it marks just the beginning of an exciting new era of successful selling for you and your company. I wish you every success.

A code of ethics for the professional salesperson

My code of ethics is to:

1 Do no harm, knowingly, to others.
2 Know and follow all relevant laws.
3 Represent my company and its products and services as truthfully and as accurately as possible.
4 Represent myself as truthfully and as accurately as possible, including all aspects of my industry knowledge, qualifications, training and experience.
5 Sell only to those customers who have a genuine requirement for my products and services.
6 Act without prejudice or bias, conflict of interest, or the undue influence of any other interested parties.
7 Carry out my duties in a manner consistent with the very highest professional standards that all customers have the right to expect.

Signed: ....

Dated: ....

index

NB: Selling skills are listed in *italic* together with their reference numbers.

presenting
amanda vickers and steve bavister

- Do you need to increase your confidence as a presenter?
- Do you want to give your presentations that extra something?
- Would you like to improve your overall powers of commuication?

Presenting shows you how to overcome nerves and bring the 'wow' factor to your presentations and public speaking. Enhanced with activities, case studies, diagrams and excerpts from famous speeches it will teach you that everything in life is a presentation but that anyone can be a successful and confident speaker.

Amanda Vickers is a Director of Speak First Limited, a training and coaching consultancy, specializing in communication skills, presenting and business relationships. **Steve Bavister** is a trainer and coach specializing in presentation skills, NLP, personal impact and communication skills.

| teach yourself | **self-motivation** |
| | frances coombes |

- Do you want to boost your creativity?
- Do you need to sharpen your motivational skills?
- Would you like to challenge your own limiting beliefs?

Self-Motivation is a simple, straightforward and inspiring guide on how to set and exceed your own goals. Including sound information from inspirational voices, this book explains what motivation is and how to define your goals, boost your creativity, create the circumstances for success and motivate others.

Frances Coombes is an NLP Master Practitioner, performance enhancement coach and expert journalist in the fields of motivation and employment.

time management
polly bird

- Do you need to maximize your time?
- Do you want to minimize your clutter and chaos at work?
- Do your days need restructuring?

Time Management shows you how to declutter your life by recording, monitoring and improving your use of time – and helps you to cut down on stress, achieve your goals, improve your performance at work and free up more time for your personal needs. It contains practical advice on prioritizing, planning your time, reducing paperwork, handling phone calls, delegating, training staff … and learning to say 'no'!

Polly Bird is a professional writer of business and training books.

| teach yourself | **NLP** |
| | steve bavister and amanda vickers |

- Are you new to Neuro-Linguistic Programming?
- Do you want to have stronger and better relationships?
- Would you like to enhance your confidence and self-esteem?

NLP gives you straightforward access to understanding one of the most powerful forms of applied psychology available today – and helps you to put the ideas and techniques into practice in your own life. This new edition also gives readers an overview of practical applications of NLP, featuring profiles and interviews with leading practitioners. If you would like to know yourself better and connect with others more easily, this is the book for you.

Steve Bavister and **Amanda Vickers** are Master Practitioners of NLP and certified NLP coaches.